The Bible's Big Story—
Our Story

Crossways International
Minneapolis, MN

THE BIBLE'S BIG STORY—*OUR STORY*
was developed and written by
Harry Wendt, Minneapolis, MN

Illustrations by Knarelle Beard, Adelaide, South Australia

The Bible text in this publication is from the New Revised Standard Version of the Bible, copyrighted 1989 by the Division of Christian Education, National Council of Churches, New York, NY, and used by permission.

THE BIBLE'S BIG STORY—*OUR STORY*
is published and distributed by
CROSSWAYS INTERNATIONAL
7930 Computer Avenue South
Minneapolis, MN 55435-5415

Contents

Introduction

Some years ago, the New Tribes Mission sent Trevor McIlwain to the Philippines to work among the Palawano people on Palawan Island. The New Tribes Mission was born with a passion for reaching people with a "simple Gospel" that required little or no training to communicate.

Soon after McIlwain began serving the Palawano people, he tried teaching them some very basic biblical doctrines, such as "Five Things You Need to Know in Order to be Saved." He got nowhere. Then he tried guiding the people through John's Gospel, verse by verse. Once again, his teaching made little or no sense to his audience. McIlwain then realized that both methods failed because the people had never been taught the basic Old Testament narrative as one complete story, as a sequence of events. So he changed his approach.

First, he decided that the Bible story itself had to be the outline. The best way to teach divine truth is to teach the biblical narrative as it unfolds in the Scriptures. The Old Testament is the *preparation for* Jesus; the New Testament is the *manifestation of* Jesus.

Second, other teaching methods are beneficial only when people have a clear panoramic view of God's dealings with humanity. In other words, understand the *story* before you try to understand the *themes*.

Third, we can learn what to emphasize from the Old Testament on the basis of what the Holy Spirit teaches and emphasizes in the New Testament; the Old Testament is the source of the themes Jesus grapples with. Jesus is the *final interpreter* of all Scripture.

Another missionary with important insights to share is Hans Rudi Weber. Weber was sent to Indonesia in 1952 by the Reformed Church to work among 30,000 nominal Christians. He was given no money and no co-workers. His helpers were the people he was sent to serve—people with an average of three years elementary education. Weber worked very successfully among his people, and drew up some fundamental principles for communicating the Christian message.

First, it is a mistake merely to tell Bible stories. Everything must be set in the context of the biblical narrative from creation to the end-time, with Jesus at the center.

Second, it is not enough to translate and teach only the New Testament or portions of the New Testament. Jesus the Messiah must not be *de-Judaized* lest He be *de-historicized.* Otherwise, Christianity runs the risk of being placed in the same category as popular myths.

What do McIlwain and Weber's conclusions mean for us today? If we want to understand the New Testament and Jesus, we should understand the story line of the Old Testament as a whole—not just fragments of it, a piece here and a piece there. The Bible is not a collection of stories about a succession of so-called heroes or a series of holy statements to be selected at random—depending on the moral point of the moment. No! The story line is a sequence of events through which is woven a series of key biblical themes. When we reach the New Testament, we must ask, "How does Jesus handle the story line? How does He reinterpret and redefine its themes?" More, we must see Jesus as the final Word of God. When we work that way, the Bible makes tremendous sense and challenges us enormously.

The time line that this booklet explains has been produced to help people put the Bible's *little stories* together in such a way that they can see the Bible's *big story.*

Harry Wendt

Harry Wendt
Minneapolis, MN

Part 1

THE TIME LINE CODES

The story that unfolds in the Bible is told from a theological and spiritual viewpoint, not a "secular" one. In many respects, it reads as a dialogue between God and His people, rather than as a diary that merely lists events. The time line tells the story of Abraham and his descendants: the Israelites and the Jews. It culminates in presenting, in brief outline, truths about the person and ministry of Jesus the Messiah.

These pages (1–3) are for reference. You will be guided through the narrative represented on the time line in Part 2.

Take out the time line from the pocket in the front cover of this book. You will find its codes explained below. (More historical background is found in Part 2 and Appendix 1.)

1. The most obvious component is a set of 22 numbered illustrations that depict key events and themes in the biblical narrative.

2. Immediately above these illustrations (beginning above illus. 2) is the center line on which are a number of figures, illustrations, numbers and symbols. Additional numbers are located on the top lines that run across the upper right section of the time line.

3. The numbers make use of a "style code" that matches the names in the top left section of the time line:

    a. Numbers in the center line: Judges [**1 2 3** etc.]; Kings; Kings/Judah [**1** **2** **3**]; Kings/Israel [1 2 3]; the Maccabees and Hasmoneans, followed by Herod the Great and Pontius Pilate [**1** **2** **3**].

    b. Numbers in the top lines: The rulers of Assyria, Babylon, Persia and Greece; the Greek Ptolemies who ruled Egypt; the Greek Seleucids who ruled Syria; Roman emperors [1 2 3].

    c. The numbers that relate to the names of the Latter Prophets are superimposed on scrolls above the center line. Note that the number "3" is placed on three scrolls. Some believe that, though Isaiah wrote all the writings that bear his name, chs. 1–39 deal with the period 742–701 B.C., chs. 40–55 speak to the Judeans in exile in Babylon, and chs. 56–66 relate to the Jews who were trying to reestablish the nation in Judah soon after they returned from Babylon. Others believe that the latter two sections were written by disciples from a "school of Isaiah" who perpetuated their master's work.

    d. The names Elijah and Elisha appear between 900 and 800 B.C.; neither prophet left anything in writing. The names of some of the postexilic prophets are not included, namely Joel, Obadiah and Jonah.

4.  Above the center line are indicators that mark off the centuries from 1900 B.C. to A.D. 200. Before the indicator for 1,900 B.C. is a small line, clock and question mark—to indicate that the length of the time-span from creation to Abraham is not known.

5. The three figures in the center line to the right of 1900 are Abraham, Sarah and Isaac.

 The four figures to the right of 1800 are Isaac, Rebekah, Jacob and Esau.

 The eighteen figures to the right of them are Jacob, his two wives and two concubines, twelve sons and one daughter.

Immediately to the right of them are an indefinite number of figures that represent the developing Jacob clan.

6. To the left of the marker for 1600 is a symbol for an Egyptian pyramid and an arrow. These serve as reminders of Jacob and his extended family settling in Egypt at the time of Joseph.

7. The symbol for covenant appears in frames 6, 11 and 14, and above frame 8. The five dots and law code represent the six parts of a covenant formula.

8. Between the markers for 1300 and 1200 is a shattered Egyptian pyramid and a simplified depiction of the Exodus from Egypt. Some interpreters believe that the Exodus took place about 1,450 B.C., two hundred years earlier than the date suggested on the time line.

9. The numbers representing the names of kings of Israel and Judah are located approximately between the markers for 1,000 and 587 B.C. Within the center line, between 1,020 and 922 B.C. (approximately), are numbers denoting the names of Saul, David and Solomon—kings who ruled a United Kingdom. The red jagged line at 922 indicates that the United Kingdom split. Between 922 and 721 B.C. are the names of the kings who ruled the Northern Kingdom of Israel. (It is not known precisely how long Saul's son, Ishbosheth, ruled the Northern Kingdom after his father's death— possibly 2–7 years; see 2 Samuel 2:10; 5:5.) Between 922 and 587 B.C. are the names of the kings who ruled the Southern Kingdom of Judah.

10. The line depicting Northern kings (922–721 B.C.) is striped vertically in magenta, blue and white (the white bands are very narrow). The changing colors indicate changes of dynasty; there were nine dynasties. The history of the Northern Kingdom came to an end when the Assyrians destroyed Israel in 721 B.C., 2 Kings 17.

11. Above the names of seven Northern kings and five Southern kings is a *dagger*. A dagger above the name of a *Northern* king indicates he was assassinated by his successor. Furthermore, Zimri committed suicide after only seven days on the throne. In relation to the *Southern Kingdom*, the dagger serves as a reminder that King Ahaziah was killed by Jehu (who later became king of the Northern Kingdom), while "the people of the land" killed four other Southern rulers: Queen Athaliah, Jehoash, Amaziah and Amon; they replaced them with a legitimate Davidic heir.

12. Superimposed on the marker for 700 B.C. is a stylized symbol of Assyrian domination: an Assyrian king and a circle of chains. The Assyrians under Sargon destroyed the Northern Kingdom in 721 B.C., and led thousands of its citizens into exile.

13. To the right of the marker for 600 is a symbol of Babylonian domination: a Babylonian *ziggurat* and circle of chains. Nebuchadnezzar finally destroyed Judah, Jerusalem and the Temple in 587 B.C. He took two kings into exile: Jehoiachin in 597 B.C., and Zedekiah in 587 B.C. Jehoiachin was still alive in 560 B.C., and 55 years of age, 2 Kings 25:27–30. Though many hoped that he would live through the exile and return to Jerusalem to reestablish the nation and the Davidic dynasty, he died in Babylon.

14. 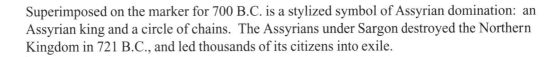 To the right of the marker for 200 is an illustration consisting of a dagger, Jerusalem, a scroll and the star of David. It serves as a reminder that, during the period 168–165 B.C., Antiochus Epiphanes of Syria persecuted the Jewish people. Though he was willing to permit them to live in Judah, he wanted to do away with Judaism and have the Jews embrace Hellenism—Greek religious ideas and the Greek way of life. Antiochus desecrated the Jerusalem Temple and insisted that every Jew should eat a small portion of pork each year. He forbade the Jews to use their scriptures, to practice circumcision, to observe Jewish festivals and the Sabbath, etc. He also demanded that all his subjects acknowledge him as divine. Through the efforts of the Maccabees (whose descendants were the Hasmoneans), the Temple was cleansed and rededicated in 165 B.C., and Judaism was reestablished. The Pharisees, initially known as the *Hasidim*, and the Sadducees appear on the scene about this time.

15. Across the upper right section of the time line are reminders of the spans of time that neighboring nations were involved in the events outlined in the biblical narrative, and symbols that depict each one:

a. Assyria

b. Babylonia

c. Persia

d. Macedonia

e. The Ptolemies

f. The Seleucids

g. The Romans

Symbols depicting the various neighboring powers are seen also on the center line above the illustrations.

 The Maccabees and their descendants, the Hasmoneans, ruled their fellow Jews from about 160–63 B.C. (This symbol is above frame 17.)

16. Above the center line, and beneath the list of nations across the top, are some red dots and dashes, names and dates. They point to key persons and events within the sweep of biblical history, though some are not alluded to in the biblical text itself. They include the following:

    a. Above the circles bearing the numbers 500, 400, and 300 are five names: Buddha, Confucius, Socrates, Plato and Aristotle. The first two are remote from the biblical narrative. The latter three were key figures in Greek history. Though they are not mentioned in the biblical narrative, they played a key role in formulating Greek thinking and religious ideas. Old and New Testament religious leaders had to respond to their teachings.

    b. The Samaritans built a temple on Mt. Gerizim some time after 332 B.C.; the Hasmoneans destroyed it in 128 B.C.

    c. The Romans under Pompey invaded Judah in 63 B.C. In 19 B.C., Herod the Great demolished the postexilic Temple and began constructing the magnificent edifice that is still referred to as "Herod's Temple." It took 82 years to build, and was completed in A.D. 63. About A.D. 66, the Jews revolted from Rome. In A.D. 70, the Romans crushed the revolt and pushed Herod's Temple off its platform into the valleys to the east and south of the building.

    d. In A.D. 64–68, Nero unleashed a persecution against the Christians, though on this occasion it was confined to Rome.

    e. In A.D. 95, Domitian unleashed a persecution that spread across the Roman Empire.

    f. The Jews revolted from Rome once again in A.D. 132 under the leadership of Bar Kochba, who was supported by Rabbi Akiba. This revolt was also put down and the Jews were now forbidden to live in Jerusalem. While these things were happening, the message of the Messiah and His Kingdom exploded out of Judea and began to spread around the Mediterranean world.

Part 2

THE TIME LINE IN DETAIL

As you read Part 2, please refer to the full-color time line in the front pocket of this book. The individual frames are reproduced in the pages that follow.

The comments below expand on the notes printed on the time line; please read the notes accompanying the appropriate frame on the color time line first.

Frames 1–3 need to be viewed as a whole, for they deal with the *biblical prologue*, Genesis 1–11. What does this imply? Though a Bible might contain, say, 1,500 pages of text, the call of Abraham is reported on perhaps page 15 in Genesis 12:1–3. Thus, one percent of the biblical message leads up to the call of Abraham, and ninety-nine percent of it follows the call of Abraham.

In short: The first eleven chapters of Genesis reveal God's purpose in bringing creation and humanity into existence (Genesis 1:1–2:4a), and describe what went wrong, Genesis 2:4b–11:9. Genesis 11:10–32 describes Abraham's roots and origins. The enormous narrative that follows describes God at work in history to form a people for a mission: to draw all people back into fellowship with God and each other, in Christ, Ephesians 1:9,10.

FRAME 1

Frame 1 is divided into five vertical segments. In the upper section of segments 2–5, two lines expand to the right, and two lines converge on the three figures representing Abraham, Sarah, and Isaac (above frame 2 on the time line). The arms of the people depicted between the expanding lines are placed on the people's hips—to depict indifference to, and rebellion against, God. As the human race grew and chaos increased, God's focus of attention narrowed down until God finally called Abraham and Sarah, Genesis 12:1–3. God's plan was to work through Abraham and Sarah to form a people through whom God would work to restore fallen creation and humanity (frame 3) to God's original intention (frame 2). God's plan of restoration was finally achieved in Jesus the Messiah (frame 20).

1. Though the Bible refers to a variety of God's attributes, the attribute that ties them together is *love*. Note the symbol for God in the time line (*black circle with four red arrows coming out from it*). The circle signifies that God is one and has no beginning or end. Because God's love always goes *out* from God to what God has made, the *four arrows depicting God's love* go *out* from God. The creation of humanity, male and female, was the high point in the process. The first humans are shown (in the very first vertical segment) with their hands raised in the posture of praise to God.

2. The lower segments numbered 2–5 depict the events described in Genesis 2–11, and the ripple effect of sin from the first humans in the garden, to their offspring in the fields, to cosmic beings, to the nations.

In segment 2, the relationship between God and humanity is broken, as is that between male and female. The serpent between the man and woman reflects the narrative outlined in Genesis 3:1–7; read also Genesis 3:8–24.

3. Genesis 4:1–6 describes the brothers Cain and Abel offering sacrifices to God. Abel's sacrifice is accepted; Cain's is not. Cain eventually kills Abel. The first murder gives rise to unbridled blood revenge, 4:17–26.

4. Genesis 6:1–4 seems to describe heavenly beings (*winged creature*) being sexually intimate with earthly women. (For other references to "sons of God," see Job 1:6, 2:1, 38:7, Psalm 82:1.) In Genesis 6:5—9:29, God instructs Noah to build an ark, through which God saves Noah and his family after sending a flood to destroy the first creation. When the waters of the flood recede, a new beginning to creation and history takes place, and a new beginning to the human race gets under way through Noah and his family.

5. Genesis 11:1–9 describes the following: People decide to build a tower (*depicted*) that will reach up into the heavens—to make a name for themselves, and to avoid being scattered. God stops the project by introducing a variety of languages (*mouth*), and by scattering the different language groups across the face of the earth.

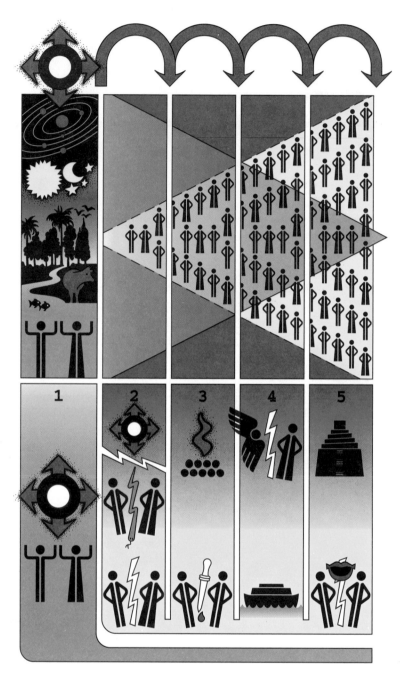

FRAME 2

1. Frame 2 depicts God's original plan for humanity. God created the universe, planet Earth and people to live on it. God's plan was that people should live to serve God by serving each other in community. Hence, superimposed on the world are two people in a kneeling, servant posture. Around the world is a circle of male and female figures, holding hands in community. A blue line runs from the bottom of frame 2 to the left and connects with the first segment of frame 1.

2. In today's Western world, considerable emphasis is placed on the importance of the *individual*. The biblical materials focus on the concept of *community*. *God's original plan* was that people were to see themselves existing *totally* to serve God by serving others in *community*.

1. The lower section of frame 3 depicts the significance of the events in Genesis 2:4b–11:32. Sin breaks in and destroys God's plan for humanity. Sin is shown as a circular arrow, signifying that people no longer serve God and others, but themselves. In five of the circles are stick figures representing people. The upper section of frame 3 shows the major narratives contained in the first eleven chapters in Genesis that describe the severing of relationships between:

   (1) God and humanity, Genesis 3.
   (2) Male and female, Genesis 3.
   (3) Brother and brother (Cain and Abel), Genesis 4,5.
   (4) The heavenly and earthly realms (cosmic chaos, perhaps), Genesis 6–9.
   (5) Nation and nation (the tower of Babel), Genesis 10,11.

2. Frame 3 and segments 2–5 of frame 1 depict what went wrong with creation and humanity. A yellow line runs from near the bottom of frame 3 to link those segments. Compare these with frame 2 and the first segment of frame 1 representing God's original plan.

3. Some of the key themes in the first eleven chapters of Genesis are:

   a. Generation—Degeneration—Regeneration.
   b. Formation—Disintegration—Restoration.

4. God made the universe and all within it to function harmoniously. It came apart. God is at work, through the Church, to put it back together again. The great Swiss theologian, Karl Barth, once said: "The Church is formed to be a provisional display of God's original intention." The Anglican Catechism defines the mission of the Church by asking a question and answering it:

   Question: *What is the mission of the Church?*

   Answer: *The mission of the Church is to restore all people to unity with God and each other, in Christ.*

   In Ephesians 1:9,10, Paul writes (RSV translation):

   God has made known to us in all wisdom and insight the mystery of his will, according to his purpose which he set forth in Christ as a plan for the fullness of time, to unite all things in him, things in heaven and things on earth.

   To see how the time line reflects these statements by Karl Barth and the Anglican Catechism, note first the original plan in frame 2, then note the chaos depicted in frame 3, and finally, in frames 19–22, see God's original intention restored in Jesus the Messiah. In Jesus' community, people are forgiven by grace, and restored to unity with God and each other.

1. Genesis 12:1–3 describes God's initial call of Abraham. When God's good creation came apart and chaos broke in among humanity at all levels, God called one man (Abraham) and one woman (Sarah), and declared that God would form a people out of them—through whom God would work to restore all people to unity with God and each other. Note the blue and purple line going from the top left of frame 4 to Abraham and Sarah (in the *circle, center line*), and Isaac standing next to them.

2. The covenant God made with Abraham was one of *Divine Commitment*. God made it. It was entirely God's doing. God promised Abraham:

   a. Land (*Israel in circle*).
   b. Offspring (*family*).
   c. The *nations would be blessed* through Abraham and his descendants. This aspect of God's covenant with the patriarchs is depicted by a *cup of blessing placed above Israel but pouring its contents over the world*. Note that Israel was formed not merely to experience blessings, but to be a means through which God might bring divine blessings to the world—ultimately in the gift of Jesus the Messiah, the Savior and Lord of humanity.

3. Above the *scroll* are a *fire-pot* and a *flaming torch*. These objects are referred to in Genesis 15:7–19, where God assured Abraham that, after 400 years, God would give Abraham's descendants the land of Canaan to dwell in. God, through the symbols of fire-pot and torch, passed between the halves of some animals Abraham had cut in two to assure Abraham that the promise concerning the land would be fulfilled. By passing between the animal halves, God was saying, "May the fate that has overtaken these animals overtake Me if I break My promise." The structure and spirit of this covenant are based on an ancient Royal Grant Treaty.

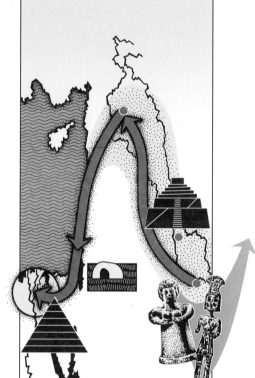

1. Frame 5 depicts events in the lives of the patriarchs: Terah, and his sons Abraham, Nahor and Haran. Haran died in Ur, Genesis 11:28. Terah and his clan eventually travelled northwest from Ur of the Chaldees (*lower right, near idols; note the ziggurat—a Babylonian sacred pyramid crowned with a temple—right center*) through the Fertile Crescent to Haran (*upper center*), where he and Abraham and their families eventually settled. (Haran was the name of a person and a place.) Terah died at Haran. According to Genesis 11:31, God called Abraham while he was living at Haran. Abraham, Sarah and Lot (Nahor's son and Abraham's nephew) then traveled south to Canaan.

2. Genesis 12:10–20 describes how, because of a drought in Canaan, Abraham and his family went south to Egypt where there was plenty of food and water. They returned to reside in Canaan. The Jacob and Joseph narratives describe how Abraham's descendants eventually moved back to Egypt (*pyramid, lower left*) and took up residence in the region of Goshen in the Nile Delta, Genesis 37–50.

3. The Genesis narrative describing the life of Abraham and Sarah contains a series of narratives designed to keep readers in suspense as they ask: Will Abraham be able to keep Sarah as his wife, 12:10–20; 20:1–18? Will Abraham and Sarah ever have children, 15:1–5; ch. 16; ch. 21; ch. 22? Will they ever gain possession of the land, ch. 13; 15:7–21; ch. 23? *The promises made in Genesis 12:1–3 are at stake throughout!*

4. Though God told Abraham that he and his descendants would receive the land of Canaan as a trust from God, at the close of his life all that Abraham owns of the Promised Land is a field and a burial cave (*lower center*) that he bought from Ephron the Hittite for 400 shekels of silver, Genesis 23.

5. Scattered throughout the narrative are stories that describe the origins of those neighboring nations that trouble and harass Israel: Canaanites, 9:25; Ishmaelites, ch. 16; Ammonites and Moabites, 19:30–38; Midianites, 25:2; Edomites, 25:19–34; Amalekites, 36:12.

6. The narrative that follows focuses on several key themes: (1) How Jacob (Isaac's son) manages to outwit his brother, Esau, 25:23; 25:29–34; ch. 27; (2) How Jacob obtains wives and his twelve sons, chs. 28–35; (3) How the people God eventually called out of Egypt first got into Egypt, chs. 37–50.

7. God did not call Abraham because of any goodness or virtue in Abraham. Joshua 24:2 states that when the Lord called the patriarchs, they were worshiping idols (*lower right; note also the blue arrow pointing to Egypt in frame 6*). Joshua 24:14,15 states that the patriarchs' descendants were still worshiping idols in Egypt just prior to the Exodus event. See also Ezekiel 20:1–9.

1. Frame 6 deals with the *key narrative* of the Old Testament: the Exodus from Egypt. At the close of the Genesis narrative, Jacob and his family are happily settled in Egypt. Some four hundred years later, at the beginning of the Exodus narrative, their descendants are in bondage there. A pharaoh arose who forgot Joseph, Exodus 1:8.

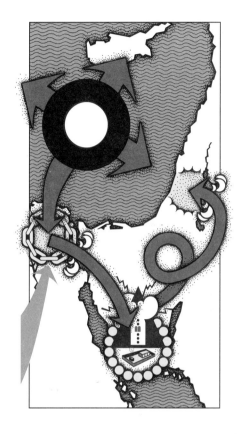

2. God broke Israel's *chains* and rescued the people from bondage. God dealt with the pharaoh through a series of plagues, led the Israelites out of Egypt (*opening up the waters* in the process), led them to *Mt. Sinai* and made a *covenant* with them, Exodus 1–20. Superimposed on Sinai is a symbol of a *covenant*; it looks like a door or a window. (A *cloud* covers the top of it.)

   Note the five dots and law code on the symbol for covenant in frames 6, 11 and 14; these represent the six parts of the covenant God made with Israel at Sinai. The structure of the Sinai Covenant reflects that of a Hittite Suzerainty Treaty between a Hittite king and a vassal (subservient) ruler—a covenant formulation which contained six parts (see point 6 below). The third section of the covenant, the stipulations or commandments, called the people to serve God and each other in *community* (*circle around Sinai*).

3. Frame 6 also shows a simplified version of *Mt. Sinai*; it looks like a triangle. Around Sinai's summit are *clouds* and *lightning*, symbolizing a *theophany*, or manifestation of God's presence, Exodus 19:16–18.

4. God then led the people *through the Sinai wilderness* to the east bank of the Jordan just to the north of the Dead Sea, Numbers 10:11–Deuteronomy 1. There God *opened up the waters once again* to lead the people *through the Jordan into the Promised Land of Canaan*, Joshua 3.

5. God did not "come down" to the top of Sinai. Rather, the symbols of the divine presence (*pillars of fire and cloud*) that led Israel out of Egypt "appeared" at the top of Sinai. These symbols of the Divine Presence then "descended" to rest above the Ark of the Covenant in the *Tabernacle*. The Ark, a treasured symbol of God's presence, was eventually placed in Solomon's Temple, 1 Kings 8:6. The Tabernacle was, in a sense, a way of making God's presence, the theophany at Sinai, *transportable*. The Tabernacle was like a portable, sacred shrine. Furthermore, the Tabernacle was virtually a half-scale model of the Temple King Solomon would build, suggesting that the Temple was thought to be so important that its layout was revealed by God to Moses on Mt. Sinai.

6. It is incorrect to define the events at Sinai as the *giving of the commandments*. Rather, God *made a covenant* with Israel at Sinai. The opening section of Exodus 20 contains major parts of this covenant formula.

(1) *Preamble*: God begins by telling the people who God is: "I am the Lord your God."

(2) *Historical Prologue*: Next, God tells the people what God has done for them: "Who brought you out of the land of Egypt, out of the house of bondage."

(3) *Stipulations*: The third part of the covenant formula consists of the collection of laws called the Ten Commandments. Exodus, Leviticus, Numbers and Deuteronomy contain other collections of stipulations.

7. There are three more parts to the covenant formula, though they are not found in Exodus 20:

(4) *Preservation and Rereading*: God tells the people to write out the covenant, preserve it and teach it to all in Israel. See Joshua 24:25,26.

(5) *Witnesses*: There are many witnesses to the covenant God has made with the people; the people must take it very seriously. See Joshua 24:27.

(6) *Blessings and Curses*: If the people take the covenant seriously, things will go well with them; if they do not, things will go badly. See Deuteronomy 28.

8. The commandments were not given to enable people to *effect* a relationship with God; rather, they were to serve as guidelines for *reflecting* a relationship with God. They were, in short, to serve as guidelines for:

(1) copying God.
(2) living in community.
(3) witnessing: to equip the Israelites to be a magnet to draw other people into God's family; see Deuteronomy 4:1–8.
(4) experiencing blessing: When people know God and do God's will, they experience inner joy and peace.

9. The covenant God made with Israel at Sinai was different from the one God made with Abraham. The covenant of *Divine Commitment* that God made with Abraham was entirely one of *promise*—one in which God stated what God would do for Abraham and his descendants *in the future*. The covenant made at Sinai was one of *Human Obligation*. In this latter covenant, God first spelled out *who God is* and *what God had done* for the people *in the past*, and then commanded the people *to respond* to God's goodness by keeping the commandments.

10. Note the white and blue line going from the top of frame 6 to the symbol for covenant in the center line.

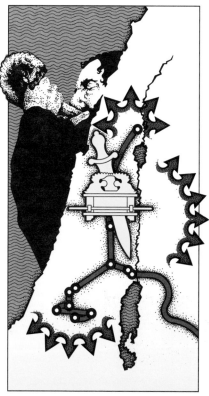

1. Frame 7 serves as a reminder of the conquest of Canaan by the Israelites under Joshua. It is outlined in the book bearing Joshua's name. It shows Joshua blowing on a *shofar* (ram's horn) to summon the people to battle. (Note the white and red line going from the top of frame 7 to the number representing Joshua's name in the center panel.) In the center of the illustration is the *Ark of the Covenant* and a *sword*. God led the people through the Jordan and into the land, symbolizing the divine presence through the Ark. Then, according to the book of Joshua, God led the people into battle against the Canaanites in a Holy War, symbolized by the sword. Preparations for the conquest are described in Joshua 1–5, the conquest itself in Joshua 6–12, and the division of the land in Joshua 13–21.

2. Some of the key thoughts in the conquest narrative are:

    a. God is the *Commander-in-chief* of Israel's armies.
    b. Joshua is God's *general*.
    c. The conquest is undertaken by a *united Israel*.
    d. The conquest is *swift* and *complete*.

3. The Joshua narrative is highly theological. The Israelite campaigns described in chs. 6, 8, 10 and 11 succeed because God devised the strategy and virtually handed victory to the Israelites on a platter. The campaign described in ch. 7 failed because the Israelites did not consult God for guidance prior to the campaign. Furthermore, because they did not consult God prior to making a treaty with the Gibeonites, God permitted them to be deceived by the latter, Joshua 9.

1. Frame 8 deals with the period of the judges. These were military leaders, whom God appointed to govern and liberate God's people. Note the yellow and red arrow going from the top right of this frame to the center line on which are listed the numbers representing names of the thirteen leaders referred to in the Book of Judges, plus that of Samuel. (The numbers correspond to the list of judges in the top left of the time line.)

2. In this panel is a symbol of the fertility gods, or weather gods, that the Israelites worshiped after they entered the land of Canaan. These images were not as large as the time line suggests. They were perhaps three to six inches high, either male or female in form, with accentuated sexual features. Beneath the image is a Canaanite farmer harvesting his crops.

3. In Egypt, the Israelites looked to the Nile for their water supply. However, after the Israelites entered the land of Canaan, they found themselves having to farm under conditions very different from what they had known in Egypt. Because there was no Nile, irrigation was not possible. The Israelites, therefore, began to join the Canaanites in their worship rituals, some of which were sexual in nature, in the hope that the "local gods" would send the rains down on their crops as well as on the Canaanites' crops, to ensure good harvests and a plentiful supply of food.

4. The formula applied to each episode describing the activities of the successive judges is given in Judges 2:11–19:

   (1) Israel sins by worshiping the Canaanite gods.
   (2) God permits a neighboring nation to harass Israel.
   (3) Israel cries for help.
   (4) God raises up a judge to deliver Israel.
   (5) Once more, Israel sins—and the cycle is repeated.

5. Judges 1:1–2:10, among other things, contains a second report of Joshua's death; see Judges 2:8,9 and Joshua 24:29,30. The first two chapters of Judges create the impression that the various tribes tried to capture the land allotted to them on an *individual basis*, tribe by tribe (the twelve tribes of Israel descended from, and were named after, Jacob's twelve sons, Genesis 46:8–24). Hence, it is possible

that the book of Joshua describes how Israel *should have* carried out the conquest, while the book of Judges reports *what actually happened*.

6. The book of Judges refers to thirteen judges from nine different tribes. Frame 8 depicts only some of the campaigns described in the narrative:

   (1) Ehud overthrew the Moabites, Judges 3:12–30.
   (2) Deborah and Barak fought the Canaanites, Judges chs. 4,5.
   (3) Gideon overcame the Midianites and Amalekites, Judges 6–8.
   (4) Jephthah defeated the Ammonites, Judges 10–12.
   (5) Samson, a Danite, did battle with the Philistines, Judges 13–16.

7. The Samson narrative actually extends to ch. 18; it was as a result of Samson's death that the Danites decided to migrate north to Laish, chs. 17,18. They took with them a priest, a shrine, and some images from Ephraim (where nevertheless "God" and "the Lord" were worshiped; note 17:2,3,13 and 18:5,6), and used them to establish a shrine in their new territory.

8. Chs. 19–21 report how wives for a remnant of the Benjaminites were obtained from Jabesh-gilead—a gruesome tale from start to finish. There are several connections between this incident and Israel's first king, Saul, a Benjaminite. It is likely that Saul's mother or wife was among the women abducted from Jabesh-gilead to become wives for the Benjaminites. Saul's relatives most likely held positions of influence there. His first royal residence was at Gibeah, the setting for the incident that sparked the decimation of the tribe of Benjamin. Saul later rescued Jabesh-gilead from the Ammonites, 1 Samuel 11. They, in gratitude, rescued the bodies of Saul and his sons from the Philistines to dispose of them in an appropriate manner, 1 Samuel 31.

9. The events outlined in Judges reveal that, if Israel wished to survive in Canaan, the tribes would have to do three things:

   a. establish *national unity*.
   b. establish a system of government with *political continuity*.
   c. establish *spiritual purity*, and do away with polytheism.

10. *Crown and question mark*: Kings: To be or not to be? That was the question!

1. Israel had been led by judges and priests. But there were continuing problems with this leadership. The five narratives describing how Israel first came to have a king are complex, 1 Samuel 8–11. Three favor having a king; two oppose the move. Throughout the debate, two words are used to describe the coming ruler: king (Hebrew, *melek*) and prince (Hebrew, *nagid*). Wherever the narrative uses the term "prince," it views the appointment favorably. On the other hand, though the term "king" can be viewed favorably, whenever the coming appointment is viewed unfavorably, the term "king" is always used. Saul is always viewed favorably in these four chapters.

    To understand the Old Testament narrative, it is very helpful to be familiar with the detailed section of Scripture that outlines the reigns of Saul, David, Solomon, Jeroboam I of Israel, and Josiah. Look for further analysis of these kings in appendices 2 and 3.

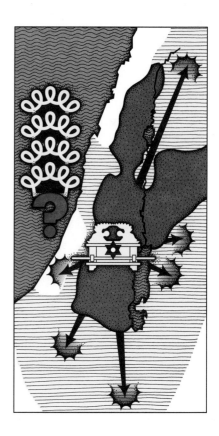

2. Eli's two sons were unfit to succeed him as priests, 1 Samuel 2:22. Samuel's two sons were also unfit to follow in their father's footsteps, 1 Samuel 8:1–3. The cry for a king went up immediately after the events described in the latter narrative.

3. The narrative outlined in Judges states that the spirit of God came upon the judges Othniel, 3:10; Gideon, 6:34; Jephthah, 11:29; and Samson, 13:25, 14:6,19, 15:14. The spirit of God came also on Israel's first king, Saul (1 Samuel 10:10, 11:6,) and King David, 1 Samuel 16:13. However, the spirit of God did not come on any king after David—when succession was determined by primogeniture. The spirit of God then came on the prophets.

4. After Saul's death, David first gained control of the Southern Kingdom of Judah, 2 Samuel 2:1–4a. A period of two or seven years passed before he gained control of the Northern Kingdom of Israel, 2 Samuel 2:10, 5:5 (it is difficult to determine the exact length from the text). After uniting the realm, David moved his capital from Hebron in central Judah to Jerusalem—on the border between Judah and Israel, 2 Samuel 5:6–10. He then brought the Ark of the Covenant to Jerusalem, and placed it into a tent he had built to house it, 2 Samuel 6. Though he expressed a desire to build a Temple to house the Ark, God told him not to do so, and told him that God would build a "house" out of David—a dynasty, 2 Samuel 7:1–17.

5. David greatly expanded his realm by conquering and annexing the Syrians to the north, the Ammonites and Moabites to the east, the Edomites to the southeast and the Amalekites to the southwest, 2 Samuel chs. 8, 10. Though he subdued the Philistines, he did not incorporate them into his realm; apparently

he employed Philistines soldiers as mercenaries to serve as his personal bodyguard, 2 Samuel 8:18, 15:18.

6. *Four crowns*: A fierce struggle to gain the throne took place among David's sons:

   (1) Amnon raped his half-sister, Tamar, and was killed by his brother, Absalom, 2 Samuel 13.
   (2) Absalom revolted from his father and declared himself king in Hebron and then Jerusalem, but was eventually killed by his cousin, Joab, 2 Samuel 15–19.
   (3) When David was well advanced in years, his son Adonijah declared himself to be king and arranged for his own coronation, 1 Kings 1:1–10.
   (4) Adonijah was eventually outsmarted by Nathan the prophet, and David's wife Bathsheba, Solomon's mother—who persuaded David to appoint Solomon as his successor, 1 Kings 1:11–2:12.

1. Frame 10 depicts key events in the reign of Solomon. Of the ten chapters 1 Kings devotes to the reign of Solomon, almost five chapters describe Solomon's building projects in Jerusalem, and most of these five chapters focus on the building and dedication of the Temple.

2. Immediately after gaining the throne, Solomon killed his brother Adonijah, exiled the priest Abiathar who (like Joab) had supported the candidacy of Adonijah for the throne, killed Joab (David's nephew and general, and therefore Solomon's cousin), and a Benjaminite, Shimei, who had cursed David when he was fleeing from Absalom, 1 Kings 2:13–46.

3. The narrative describing Solomon's reign suggests that the Temple would stand forever (1 Kings 8:13), and that Jerusalem was the place where God had chosen to make God's name to dwell, 1 Kings 8:16; but note also Jeremiah 7:12, where the prophet states that God made God's name to dwell at first in Shiloh.

4. The word "if" shows up frequently in the narrative that describes Solomon's reign, and makes virtually every previous promise conditional. If the king and people do not walk in the ways of David (i.e., worship one God in one Temple in one city, Jerusalem), they will lose their status as God's people, 1 Kings 6:11–13; the Davidic dynasty, 1 Kings 9:4,5; the land, 9:6,7; and the Temple, 9:8,9.

5. The conditional nature of God's promise was reiterated by the prophet Micah, writing about 200 years later, who stated in no uncertain terms that Jerusalem and the Temple would be destroyed; he based his attack on the failure of the people to take seriously the Sinai covenant, Micah 3:9–12; 6:1–8.

6. Though in 1 Kings 10 the writer takes great delight in describing the lavish nature of Solomon's building ventures, 1 Kings 14:23–25 points out that the Egyptians plundered Jerusalem and the Temple five years after Solomon's death, stripped the buildings of their gold and treasures, and took them as booty back to Egypt. So much for the "splendor" of Solomon's reign!

7. Though Solomon is often referred to as one of the biblical "greats" in literature produced for popular consumption (he built the *Temple*, top left), the truth is that he exploited and enslaved his people (*lower right*), particularly the northern part of his realm, to satisfy his personal ambitions and comfort level (*center right*).

8. *Women, idols, question marks*: 1 Kings 11:3 states that Solomon had 700 wives and 300 concubines. No doubt, many of these marriages were undertaken to establish and maintain good political relationships with neighboring nations. The writer never attacks Solomon for having numerous wives; he attacks him for worshiping the false gods of those wives, 1 King 11:1–8.

9. Above frame 10 is a yellow circle shaded with sloping black lines. To its right is the explanatory comment, "Did that which was right in the sight of the Lord—worshiped one God in one place, Jerusalem." Similar sloping lines are superimposed on the segments of the center line denoting the reigns of David, Solomon, and eight more Southern kings. Those wishing to make sense out of the biblical narrative must understand the message of 1 Kings 11:4–6, which refers to David as being wholly true to the Lord his God for the simple reason that he *worshiped one God in one place, Jerusalem*!

    Note also the reference to 1 Samuel 13:14, where soon-to-be-anointed David is referred to as a person "after God's own heart." The term does not refer to any moral superiority on David's part. It means simply that David would, and did, worship one God in one city, Jerusalem. Hence, any successor who paid special attention to the Jerusalem Temple (which David's son, Solomon, built) is described as one who did what was right, who walked in the way of David his father, and departed neither to the right hand nor to the left; see 2 Kings 22:2.

10. *Crowned king, with servant person on each side*: Solomon established a realm in which the people were organized to serve the king.

11. *Divided crown with servant figures*: Saul, David and Solomon had ruled a United Kingdom. Because Solomon ruled his people harshly, immediately after his death the United Kingdom of Israel split into two sections:

    a. The Northern Kingdom of Israel.
    b. The Southern Kingdom of Judah.

12. Nineteen kings from nine dynasties ruled the Northern Kingdom, Israel. With one exception, each new dynasty took over from the previous dynasty by killing the king on the throne, which meant seven assassinations in all. The one exception was Zimri, who committed suicide after only seven days on the throne, thus saving Omri the trouble of having to kill him.

    After Solomon's death, a total of nineteen kings and one queen (Athaliah) ruled Judah. Though five of these rulers were assassinated, the assassination never meant a change in dynasty; the same family continued to rule. To be specific, Jehu of the Northern Kingdom killed Ahaziah. The queen mother, Athaliah, a daughter of Ahab and Jezebel, then killed her grandchildren and grabbed the throne; unbeknown to her, one grandson, Joash, was hidden away in the Temple by the High Priest and his wife (Joash's aunt). The people of the land eventually killed Athaliah, replaced her with Joash, but eventually killed Joash and his son Amaziah, and finally Manasseh's son, Amon.

13. The Davidic dynasty continued until the Southern Kingdom of Judah was destroyed by the Babylonians in 587 B.C. The second-to-last king, Jehoiachin, died in Babylon some time after 560 B.C. In 2 Kings 25:27–30, reference is made to the thirty-seventh year of the exile of Jehoiachin, who was taken to Babylon in 597 B.C. Whoever wrote those words must have written them during or after the year 560 B.C.

1. Frame 11 depicts the prophetic attack. Many today think that the ancient prophets merely foretold the future. Though they did some of that, they were *forth*-tellers rather than *fore*-tellers. In other words, they *spoke forth* for God to the people of their own time and attacked them on the basis of the Sinai covenant (*shown broken, lower left*).

2. The biblical materials state that the spirit of God came upon prophets who, with a wind in their beards and a fire in their eyes, told kings, leaders, and "professional" priests and prophets that they were to live under the Sinai covenant and serve the nation in a manner that was in keeping with its spirit and stipulations. They told both the leaders and people that they had forgotten God's goodness and mercy, and charged them with serving personal whims rather than God's will, Hosea 13:4–6.

(1) They robbed each other in business dealings, Amos 8:4–6 (*scales*). All that political and religious leaders worried about was how much money they could make for themselves, Micah 3:9–11 (*mouth and dollar sign*). Those in charge of the legal system exploited the poor to fill their own pockets, Amos 5:10,11 (*gavel and dollar sign*).

(2) Though God was merciful and patient, there was a limit to God's patience. God would maul them like a lion, like a leopard, like a bear robbed of her cubs, Hosea 13:7,8 (*leopard*). God would permit the Egyptians, Assyrians and Babylonians to ravage their land, fortresses, cities, towns and homes, Hosea 9:6; Jeremiah 27:1–6 (*buildings reduced to rubble*).

(3) At the same time, the prophets expressed the hope that, after disciplining the nation, God would make a new beginning to their history as God's people. They hoped that God would make a new covenant with His people and write it on their hearts (*lower right*) so that they might be a people who truly *knew* their God, Jeremiah 31:31–34.

Despite the hopes and dreams of Israel and Judah, and the beliefs each entertained about its destiny in relation to God's covenant and plan, both nations were eventually destroyed (*city in flames*), and their leaders and many citizens were led into exile (*people tied to each other*) into foreign lands (*ziggurat*).

A.   ASSYRIA (*profile of Assyrian king*)

1. The first magenta-colored section in the top line of the time line denotes the Assyrian Empire. One of the reasons Saul, David and Solomon were able to achieve what they did was that they did not have to cope with any real threats from the Egyptians to the south or the Assyrians to the north.

2. However, as time went by, the Assyrians began to flex their muscles. Eventually, they made the Northern Kingdom a vassal nation, destroyed it in 721 B.C., and scattered many of its citizens around their vast Empire—hence *the red arrow going from Israel to Assyria*, 2 Kings 17. To force captives to cooperate when being led into exile, the Assyrians ran a *fish hook* through the nose of each person and linked the hooks together with cord.

3. The Assyrians intermarried those left behind with non-Israelites brought in from around their extensive empire. These "mixed bloods" became known as the Samaritans. The Samaritans accepted the Pentateuch (Genesis—Deuteronomy) as their Scriptures, believed in the same God as the Jews, but worshiped that same God on *Mt. Gerizim*—not on *Mt. Zion* in *Jerusalem*. In Jesus' conversation with the woman of Samaria, reference is made to these rival worship places, John ch. 4; see also Luke 9:51–56.

B.   BABYLON (*ziggurat*)

1. By the time of the death of Shalmaneser V in 627 B.C., the Assyrian Empire was hearing its own death rattle. The Babylonians finally conquered Assyria, overthrowing Asshur in 614 B.C. and Nineveh in 612 B.C. Though the Egyptians gained control of Judah in 609 B.C., in 605 B.C. the Babylonians defeated Egypt in battle and Judah became a vassal of Babylon.

2. King Jehoiakim of Judah revolted against Babylon in 601 B.C. King Nebuchadnezzar of Babylon put down the revolt in 597 B.C.; after King Zedekiah of Judah revolted in 589, Nebuchadnezzar finally destroyed Judah, Jerusalem, the Temple and the Ark of the Covenant in 587 B.C., 2 Kings 24,25. Though the Babylonians left some people in Judah, they took the royal family and thousands of the nobility and leading citizens into exile in Babylon; hence, *the arrow from Judah to Babylon.*

3. The Persians under Cyrus captured Babylon in 539 B.C. and replaced the Babylonian Empire as the ranking empire in the Fertile Crescent. Cyrus pursued an enlightened policy. He permitted captive peoples to return home and rebuild their communities and temples. Hence, the exiles from Judah began to return to their homeland in 538 B.C.; *note the arrow from Babylon to Judah.* Those who returned

to Judah, or Judea, were called "Judeans," or "Jews" for short. They began and developed that system of belief known still today as "Judaism"; note the word "Judaism" beneath the marker for 300 B.C.

FRAME 13

1. Those taken into exile in Babylon experienced an agony of spirit (*sorrowful faces*). They were being forced to live away from what they thought of as the Holy Land, the Holy City and the Holy Temple. They were being forced to sing the Lord's song in a strange land, Psalm 137.

2. Many of them came to understand that they had truly deserved what had overtaken them, for they had indeed broken God's covenant with them. A prophet pointed out that through their suffering, healing and salvation would flow out to all peoples (*concentric circles radiate out from Israel*). God had formed Israel to be a servant community (*servant figure, lower right*), through whom the light of God's truth (*lamp*) would be made known to the nations, Isaiah 42:1–4, 49:1–6; 50:4–11; 52:13–53:12.

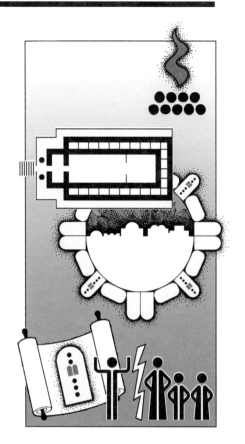

Those who went back from Babylon to Judah thought that they would go back to experience the Messianic Age—that the land to which they would return would be virtually a new Eden, Isaiah 51:1–3. When they got back, there was no Eden and no Messianic Age—but a mess.

Because the land, Jerusalem and the Temple were in ruins, the people had to undertake the slow, laborious task of rebuilding them and reestablishing themselves as a community within Judah. They had to do that, for there was only one God; because only the Jews knew and belonged to that God, they were to make that God known to the nations.

1. *Altar*: The exiles began to return from Babylon to Judah in 538 B.C. They soon built an altar and began offering sacrifices, Ezra 3:1–6.

2. *Temple*: The prophets Haggai and Zechariah (chs. 1–8) encouraged them to rebuild the Temple. The postexilic Temple was dedicated in 515 B.C., Ezra 6:13–18.

3. *Bricks in circle around Jerusalem*: Nehemiah spearheaded the move to rebuild Jerusalem's walls, Nehemiah chs. 2,3. He also arranged for more people to live in Jerusalem (ch. 11), established laws forbidding the rich and powerful to exploit the poor (5:1–13), and reinstituted Sabbath observance, 13:15–22.

4. *Symbols for covenant and commandments in circle around Jerusalem; also scroll with symbol for covenant*: The postexilic community became increasingly narrow in its territorial, national and religious outlook. After Ezra returned from Persia to Jerusalem, he instructed the people in the law of the Lord, and conducted a covenant-renewal ceremony.

5. *Symbol for fragmented family*: Though Nehemiah had forbidden Jewish men to contract marriages with non-Jewish women, he did not break any existing Jewish-Gentile marriages, Nehemiah 13:23–29. However, Ezra insisted that all Jewish men married to non-Jewish women dissolve those marriages, and send their Gentile wives and their children away from the restored Jewish community, Ezra chs. 9,10. The intention was to ensure the religious purity of the postexilic community by removing foreign elements. The people remembered only too well how Solomon's many foreign wives had influenced the spiritual life of the nation, 1 Kings 11:1–8.

6. The peoples and nations surrounding Judah generally resented the Jews' attempt to reestablish themselves in the land, and harassed them, Nehemiah 4.

1. *Symbol for God, crown, question mark*: Jehoiakim of Judah, who revolted against Babylon in about 601 B.C., died approximately three months before the city fell in 597 B.C. He was replaced by his 18 year-old son, Jehoiachin, whom Nebuchadnezzar took into exile. Though many of the exiles hoped that Jehoiachin would live through the exile, return to Jerusalem, and reestablish the Davidic dynasty (2 Kings 25:27–30), Jehoiachin died in Babylon— as did also his successor, Zedekiah, whose sons were killed and who was blinded and taken into exile in 587 B.C.

2. The postexilic community had no king—apart from God who ruled the people through the priests and maintained fellowship with them through the rituals the priests performed in the rebuilt Jerusalem Temple. Even so, many in the postexilic community hoped that God would eventually restore the Davidic dynasty.

3. Though the postexilic community was able to reestablish itself as a people within the land, and to rebuild Jerusalem, its walls and the Temple, they did not have political independence. They remained, in turn, vassals of the Persians (*winged cherub*), the Greeks, Ptolemies and Seleucids (*helmet and sword*), and finally the Romans. To complicate matters, their Greek overlords (including the Ptolemies, and in particular the Seleucids) made efforts to impose their own culture and way of life (Hellenism, *column*) on them. Little wonder, then, that the agonizing cry went up, "Oh Lord, when will you restore the Davidic dynasty and the kingdom of David?"; see Psalm 89. (Refer to Appendix 1.)

1. The names of many of Israel's prophets are given in the time line, beginning with Elijah and Elisha. Though the ministries of Elijah and Elisha (900–800 B.C.) are reported in 1 Kings 17–2 Kings 10, no writings bearing their names have come down to us.

2. The literary prophets listed are Amos, Hosea, Isaiah of Jerusalem, Micah, Nahum, Habakkuk, Zephaniah, Jeremiah and Ezekiel—in that order and all prior to the Babylonian exile or during its first years. Jeremiah began his work in 626 B.C., and was still active in 582 B.C. Ezekiel was called in 593 B.C. while in Babylon, and his final oracle is dated about 571 B.C.

3. Next comes the book that is usually referred to as Second Isaiah (and *possibly* a Third Isaiah), followed by Haggai, Zechariah and Malachi. Note that the names of Obadiah, Joel and Jonah are not listed on the time line. Then, no more literary prophets. Why not?

4. The answer is given in frame 16. The people became *the people of the book.* They believed there was no further need for the voice of a living prophet. Everything the people needed to know, believe and do was now available to them in written form. Jewish scholars studied their writings in great detail; as time went by, they produced supplementary writings to explain and apply the law codes, in particular to the life of the postexilic community. Hence, frame 16 (*lower section*) contains a *scroll* with a center block of inspired writing, around which are comments on the biblical text by interpreters (*arrows pointing to central text*). See also Zechariah 13:2–6.

5. *Portion of bread, drop of water, lamp*: Jewish rabbis spoke of their sacred writings as the bread of life, the water of life and the light of the world. Eventually, Jesus, the Final Word of God, applied these terms to His Person, teachings and work, John chs. 4, 6 and 9.

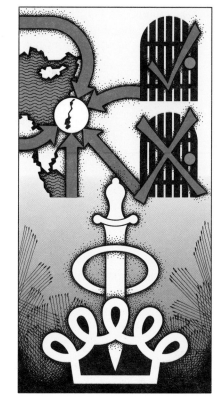

1. *Crown, halo, sword*: The members of the postexilic community entertained a variety of hopes. Many, though not all, believed that a Messianic Age would eventually break in. Many, though again not all, believed that the Messianic Age would come about through the efforts of a righteous king descended from David, Isaiah 9:1–7, 11:1–9. Still others looked for the coming of a divine king who would destroy the Gentile nations (frequently in the prophetic "doom oracles," Isaiah chs. 13–23; Jeremiah chs. 46–51; Ezekiel chs. 25–32; Zechariah chs. 9–14; Daniel 7) and establish the (Jewish) kingdom of God over the world—or at least, over the world as the writers understood it at that time. (See also *Psalms of Solomon* 17 and 18, written by the Pharisees about 50 B.C. Note also Jesus' radical "editing" of Isaiah 61:1–7 in Luke 4:16–30.)

2. *Arrows pointing to Israel*: Some believed that, when the Messianic Age broke in, Jewish people scattered around the Near Eastern world would return to Israel to take part in it.

3. *Slatted door, signifying resurrection, with approval sign*: The Pharisees, whose origins can be traced to the *Hasidim* who appear about 160 B.C., believed that when the Messianic Age broke in, the righteous dead would return to life to take part in it, Isaiah 25:8, 26:19; Daniel 12:1–3.

4. *Slatted door, signifying resurrection, with rejection sign*: The Sadducees, whose origins can also be traced to about 160 B.C., did not believe in any future Messianic Age or the resurrection of the body, Acts 23:8

1. *Temple*: The postexilic Temple was dedicated in 515 B.C. In 19 B.C., King Herod the Great, with the approval of Jewish religious and political leaders, demolished the existing building and replaced it with one of magnificent proportions. The structure, completed in A.D. 63, was destroyed by the Romans in A.D. 70.

2. *Law code with "613" superimposed*: The law codes in the first five books of the Old Testament (the Pentateuch) were theoretically given to a nation living in the Sinai wilderness after leaving Egypt. These consisted of the original ten commandments (or "words"), plus an additional 603 commandments that rabbis, or teachers, found in these writings—making a total of 613.

3. *Smaller law codes around the larger law code*: Because the people felt the need to make these law codes relevant to their new and ever-changing situation, scribes adapted and reinterpreted them for later generations. In due course, a collection of oral teachings developed which became known as the traditions of the scribes and Pharisees.

   Hundreds of years later, these oral traditions were written down in several collections of writings: The *Mishnah*, *Gemara*, *Tosefta*, *Midrashim* and the *Talmuds*. The *Palestinian Talmud*, produced at Tiberias, was completed about A.D. 400, and the *Babylonian Talmud* was completed about A.D. 500. The Babylonian Talmud is about twice as large as the Palestinian Talmud.

FRAME 19: JESUS, THE PIVOTAL POINT OF BIBLICAL HISTORY

Finally, the events described in the New Testament began to unfold. On the vertical strip separating the Old Testament from the New Testament sections of the time line are symbols of Jesus' birth (*crib*), servant life, crucifixion, burial and resurrection. The *tomb* is open and empty, signifying Jesus' return to life and continuing presence as King among His people.

Jesus, complete with basin and towel, is depicted as a Servant-King surrounded by a community. This illustration is based on a number of biblical passages:

1. the words spoken at Jesus' baptism: "You are my Son, the Beloved; with you I am well pleased," Mark 1:9–11.

    "You are my Son, the Beloved," is found in verse 7 of Psalm 2, a royal psalm. It was used when a king from the line of David was enthroned. Its use at Jesus' baptism indicates He was anointed King of God's people (*crown*).

    "With you I am well pleased" is found in the first of Isaiah's Servant Songs (Isaiah 42:1–4); its use at Jesus' baptism tells us God declared Him a servant (*servant figure*).

2. According to John 13:1–17, during the night prior to His crucifixion, Jesus washed His disciples' feet and told them that they were to do the same for each other.

3. Around Jesus is a community. During His ministry, Jesus gathered around Himself a group of people, a community. In His Kingdom, all distinctions between male and female, one race and another, master and servant, were and are superseded, irrelevant and rejected. Each one of Jesus' followers is to ask only: "How can I reflect Jesus' attitude toward the Father, toward the created order and toward others?"

4. Above the illustration is a dove, the symbol for the Holy Spirit. The risen, ascended Jesus continues among His people through His Spirit. The Spirit continues the work of Jesus. Their work is one and inseparable, John 16:14,15.

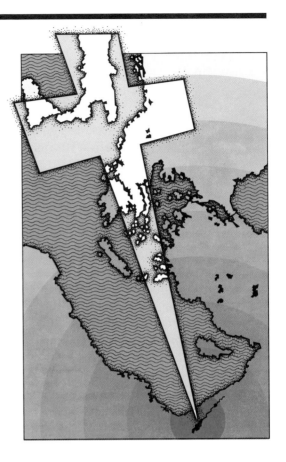

1. Until the very day of Jesus' ascension, the disciples hoped that Jesus would restore the Davidic kingdom—one that was political in nature. Jesus rejected this expectation, Acts 1:6–8.

2. Furthermore, Jesus told the disciples that the Holy Spirit would soon empower them to witness about Jesus to those living in Jerusalem, Judea and Samaria; beyond that, they would carry the message to the ends of the earth, Acts 1:8.

3. Though many Jews hoped to see a Messianic Age established in Judea and centered on Jerusalem, Jesus sent people away from Jerusalem to distant horizons. Some Jews hoped that even Romans would come to worship the God of the Jews in Jerusalem, but at the close of the Book of Acts (ch. 28), Paul is bearing witness to Jesus in Rome. In short, the world was not won for God by zealot swords, but by the message and mission of a gentle Galilean.

The New Testament says that Jesus the Messiah will reappear on a day that will mark the close of history, Matthew 25:31–46.

1. On that day, Jesus will separate humanity into two groups—sheep at His right hand, goats at His left hand.

    He will welcome those at His right hand (those blessed by His Father), and invite them to inherit the kingdom prepared for them from the foundation of the world, Matthew 25:31–40. He will also reject those who claimed to know Him as Lord, but whose faith was false in that it did not demonstrate itself in service to the needy, Matthew 25:41–46. Though the Bible proclaims that salvation is always "by grace, through faith" in Jesus the Messiah, crucified, risen and reigning, it always attaches the concept of "for works, for servanthood" to "by grace, through faith," Ephesians 2:8–10. Faith in the heart demonstrates itself in service by the hands.

2. Though Jesus will finally receive people into eternal fellowship with Himself on the basis of the gracious forgiveness of sins, He will commend them for works of service they did to the needy around them—and through them, to Jesus Himself in "distressing disguise." He will thank them for providing for His needs when He was hungry (*plate, knife and fork*), thirsty (*drinking glass*), lonely (*one person separated from three other persons*), lacking clothing, sick (*serpent around a staff*—symbol for healing, Numbers 21:1–9) and in *prison*. Jesus will also reject those who claimed the right to call Him "Lord," but failed to serve Him in His multitude of distressing disguises, Matthew 25:41–46.

3. *Meal, signified by food and drink on the table (left):* Jesus frequently ate with people. In Jesus' day, to eat with people was to accept them warmly as brothers and sisters. It was to establish a sense of sacred community with them.

    Basin and towel (right): Jesus performed the duties of a servant for His disciples; He washed their feet. He exhorted them, and exhorts His family today, to copy Him—to make the present but invisible Jesus visible through word and actions, John 13:1–17.

    Wafer and chalice (center): Prior to His final appearing, Jesus continues among His people, invisibly, through His Spirit. He invites them to share table with Him (as He shared table with His disciples during His earthly ministry), and gives them Himself to eat and drink through visible elements of bread and wine. Those who share sacramental table fellowship with Him are to "become" what they eat. They are to demonstrate in their own lives the life of Jesus, their Savior, Lord and Master.

AND FINALLY...

The following paragraph was written by H.G. Wells. Its implications are timeless.

Jesus was too great for His disciples. And in view of what He plainly said, is it any wonder that all who were rich and prosperous felt a horror of strange things, a swimming of their world at His teaching? Perhaps the priests and rulers and rich men understood Him better than His followers. He was dragging out all the little private reservations they had made from social service into the light of a universal religious life. He was like a terrible moral huntsman, digging mankind out of the snug burrows in which they had lived hitherto. In the white blaze of His kingdom there was to be no property, no privilege, no pride and no precedence, no motive and reward but love. Is it any wonder that men were dazzled and blinded, and cried out against Him? Even His disciples cried out when He would not spare them that light. Is it any wonder that the priests realized that between this Man and themselves there was no choice, but that He or their priestcraft should perish? Is it any wonder that the Roman soldiers, confronted and amazed by something soaring over their comprehension and threatening all their disciplines, should take refuge in wild laughter, and crown Him with thorns and robe Him in purple and make a mock Caesar of Him? For to take Him seriously was to enter into a strange and alarming life, to abandon habits, to control instincts and impulses, to essay an incredible happiness. Is it any wonder that to this day this Galilean is too much for our small hearts?

— *The Outline of History, Vol. 1, pp. 425–6*

Part 3

THE MAJOR THREADS

1. Genesis 1–11 explains God's purpose in calling Abraham, in that God's original and good plan (frame 2) gave way to moral chaos (frame 3) on a cosmic scale. Abraham was to be the first of a people through whom God would work to restore the original plan (frame 2).

2. There are indications that some saw the promise to Abraham (frame 4) fulfilled in David's kingdom (frame 9); others saw it fulfilled in the Northern Kingdom that was established after King Solomon's death. (The United Kingdom split into the Northern Kingdom, Israel, and the Southern Kingdom, Judah.)

3. A major thread that runs through the narrative relates to the pre-exilic prophets. The prophets almost invariably attacked the religious and sacrificial system revolving around the shrines and the Jerusalem Temple. They said that the people had broken the Sinai covenant with abandon, forgotten God's goodness, and ignored the plight of the needy—such as the widows and orphans. They warned that judgment was imminent and would prove devastating. Few listened!

4. The Assyrians destroyed the Northern Kingdom in 721 B.C. Those who wrote the biblical record stated that God permitted the Assyrians to destroy Israel because of the latter's polytheism, 2 Kings 17. For some of the reasons the biblical writers offer for the destruction of Judah by the Babylonians, see 2 Kings 23:4–14.

5. Some believed that, with King Josiah (640–609 B.C., 2 Kings 22,23), the Davidic kingdom was being restored, 2 Kings 23:25. Josiah was a descendant of David; he reigned in Jerusalem over Judah, declared independence from Assyria, established control over the former Northern Kingdom, and centralized worship in the Jerusalem Temple. However, after Josiah was killed by the Egyptians in 609 B.C. (2 Kings 23:28–30), Judah was ruled by the Egyptians until 605 B.C., when the Babylonians took over. After King Jehoiakim of Judah rose up against Babylon in 601 B.C., King Nebuchadnezzar of Babylon crushed the revolt in 597 B.C. After a second revolt by King Zedekiah in 589 B.C., Nebuchadnezzar destroyed Judah, Jerusalem and the Temple in 587 B.C. Two Judean kings were taken into exile: Jehoiachin in 597 B.C. and Zedekiah in 587 B.C., 2 Kings 23:31–25:30.

6. The exiles in Babylon agonized over why their history had apparently come to an end. Those who completed the writing of Joshua through 2 Kings suggested, among other things, that the nation was destroyed because the people had worshiped many gods, and had not worshiped one God in one place, Jerusalem, as David had done. Therefore, if the people ever returned to Judah and Jerusalem, they must "walk in the ways of David."

7. After the Persians overthrew Babylon in 539 B.C., some of the exiles returned to Judah to reestablish themselves there. Only those who had taken part in the exile could belong to "God's new people"— which focused its attention on the restored Temple and its rituals, and on the observance of the law codes. Now without kings, they longed for the time when God would restore the Davidic dynasty and kingdom, pour divine vengeance on the Gentile nations, and establish Abraham's descendants as the rulers of the world, Psalm 89, Isaiah 13–23, Jeremiah 46–51, Daniel 7.

8. The Kingdom Jesus established proved to be very different from what the people of His day were expecting!

JESUS, THE FINAL INTERPRETER OF SCRIPTURE

The Bible is a complex library that took more than a thousand years to write. It grapples with a long and complicated history—a history whose "grand finale" took place in the mission and ministry of Jesus the Messiah. Hebrews 1:1–3 states:

> Long ago God spoke to our ancestors in many and various ways by the prophets,
> but *in these last days he has spoken to us by a Son* whom he appointed heir of
> all things, through whom he also created the worlds. He is the reflection of
> God's glory and the exact imprint of God's very being, and he sustains all things
> by his powerful word. [emphasis added]

Because the Word of God finally became a Person in Jesus, we need to read Jesus' lips and life.

A.   THE ILLUSTRATION IN OUTLINE

On a number of occasions, the Bible describes God revealing the divine presence through the symbol of a cloud: during the Exodus and wilderness wanderings, at Sinai, and at the dedication of Solomon's Temple. On the cloud is the symbol for God that you have seen on the time line. (The circle signifies that God is One and has no beginning or end. The arrows indicate that love always goes out from God.)

Then a line runs down, and up, and down again. On that line are some symbols—about thirteen in all. At the end of that line is an arrow that points to a funnel. On the funnel is Jesus. All Old Testament themes must be funneled through Jesus' mind and teaching. Jesus is in the posture of a servant wearing a crown. At His baptism, Jesus was declared to be King and Servant, Mark 1:9–11; Psalm 2:7; Isaiah 42:1. Behind Jesus is a cross. Jesus walked the way of a servant without limit, to the point of giving away life itself to save sinful humanity from the power of Satan, sin and eternal death. The irony is that when Jesus appeared to be at His weakest, He was at His strongest, for His cross was His throne. His resurrection was His vindication by His Heavenly Father. His ascension was His enthronement over the universe.

Beneath the funnel are two people, facing each other in a servant posture. Jesus gathered around Himself a community of believers who were to live as He lived—to walk the way of a servant without limit, in fellowship with each other and the world of humanity. Blessedness is measured by what people give of themselves in the service of others.

In what follows, the numbers correspond to those in the illustration. Reference is made *first* to how the Old Testament and Judaism interpreted the concepts listed, and *second* to how Jesus finally interpreted them.

1. *The people of God*: The four people represent the first of the so-called "chosen people," namely, the patriarchs Abraham and Sarah, Isaac and Rebekah. God had made a covenant of divine commitment with Abraham. God promised Abraham that God would make a people out of him and Sarah, Genesis 12:1–3. In Jesus' day, the Jews taught and believed that only they knew and belonged to God. To belong to God, one must be born of a Jewish womb.

    Jesus taught: Jesus was descended from Abraham. Though, in Jesus, the history of God's people continues, it nevertheless experiences a radical new beginning. Jesus insists that membership in His new people has nothing to do with physical descent from Abraham. Racial roots and origins count for nothing. People are born into God's family through water and the Spirit. All who trust in Jesus as Savior, and follow Him as Lord, are members of God's true people, Galatians 3:27–29. They are received into the kingdom of God by virtue of the Father's forgiving grace—declared finally and gloriously at the cross and empty tomb!

2. *The Promised Land*: Note a portion of the Mediterranean Sea to the left, the Sea of Galilee to the north, the Dead Sea to the south, the Jordan River flowing between them, and the location of Jerusalem marked with a circle. God told the patriarchs God would eventually grant them the right to live in Canaan as God's tenants. In the Old Testament, the "Holy Land" plays a key role in salvation history and is the focal point of Israel's hopes and dreams.

Jesus taught: Christians can look forward, in faith and hope, to the time when they will enter an eternal inheritance—heaven itself. Though the land of Israel or Palestine intrigues Christians historically, it certainly is not the focus of their hopes; see 1 Peter 1:3–5.

3. *Circle of chains; arrow breaking through those chains*: God rescued the Israelites from bondage in Egypt, and later God rescued those Israelites who were taken into exile in Babylon, enabling them to return to Judah and Jerusalem.

Jesus taught: Christians are rescued from their real enemies (Satan, sin and eternal death) by Jesus' sinless life, death and resurrection. Jesus forgives His brothers and sisters what they have done, teaches them to walk as He walked, and promises them eternal life—now and forever, Romans 6:1–5.

4. *Mt. Sinai, theophany, symbol for covenant with commandments superimposed*: After God rescued the Israelites from Egypt, God led them to Mt. Sinai and showed God's presence among them through a storm cloud. At Sinai, God made a covenant with Israel. The symbol for a covenant looks a little like a door or a window. In the covenant, God told the Israelites who God was and is, what God had done for them in the past, and how they were to respond in obedience.

Jesus taught: The awesome presence, heart and will of God are revealed in Jesus' person and through His teaching, John 14:8–11. When Jesus was transfigured in the presence of the disciples, He was surrounded by a bright cloud and light—symbols that declared Jesus to be the God of the Old Testament, Exodus 24:15–18; Luke 9:28–36.

When Jesus shared the bread and wine with the disciples in the Upper Room, He declared the Sinai covenant to be superseded, and His new covenant to be established, Luke 22:20.

In Galatians 3:24,25, Paul, too, says that the Old Testament revelation given at Sinai is superseded. It was designed to serve only on a short-term, temporary basis. Paul refers to its function as a *paidagogos* (in Greek), which English Bibles translate variously as custodian, disciplinarian, schoolmaster, etc. The best translation of *paidagogos* is "nanny."

Wealthy people sometimes employ women to serve as a nanny to care for their children while they pursue their own careers or social life. The nanny dresses the children, feeds them, takes them to school, gets them home at the end of the day, supervises their homework and so forth. But when the children grow up, the nanny's services are no longer needed.

Similarly, the Old Testament revelation given at Sinai had a short-term function. It no longer "supervises" us Christians. We live under Jesus the Messiah. Jesus is our Truth, Law, Revelation and Teaching.

The pattern for the life Christians are to pursue is Jesus' life. They are to think, speak and serve as Jesus thought, spoke and served, John 13:12–15,34,35. The commandments listed in the New Testament writings serve as guidelines for Christians as they seek to make visible the invisible Jesus who remains among them.

5. *Female image representing the fertility gods the Israelites worshiped in Canaan*: Those who worshiped the Canaanite gods sought to control the weather patterns to ensure good rains, bountiful crops and a sure food supply!

   Jesus taught: Jesus pointed out that wherever people's treasure is, their heart will be also, Matthew 6:21. The gods people worship today in affluent countries are different from those the Canaanites worshiped. People today are influenced by many false gods; their bank accounts, shopping malls, homes and garages are stuffed with them. John Calvin said that the human mind is an idol factory. Martin Luther said that whatever people devote their life to is their god.

6. *The Ark of the Covenant*: The Ark of the Covenant was a symbol of God's presence among the Israelites, Deuteronomy 10:1–5. It led the Israelites during the wilderness wanderings and through the Jordan into Canaan where it was eventually placed into Solomon's Temple. The Babylonians destroyed it in 587 B.C.

   Jesus taught: Jesus, God's presence, remains among God's people. The Risen Jesus did not withdraw His presence; He merely transformed it. Jesus continues among His people invisibly; He speaks to them through written and spoken words that touch their eyes and ears, and through sacraments that touch their bodies.

   Sword: After the Israelites entered Canaan, they carried out a "holy war" (*sword*) against the Canaanites. That holy war was a rather brutal affair.

   Jesus taught: Christians are to fight against that "deadly trio" Luther called "the devil, the world and the sinful flesh." This "unholy trio" wants Christians to serve themselves, rather than God and others; see Ephesians 6:10–18.

7. *Crown*: Though, after the conquest, the Israelites were ruled by judges, they eventually appointed a king—first Saul, and then David. God had made a covenant of Divine Commitment (promise) with David. God promised David that God would make a line of kings (or dynasty) out of him and his descendants, 2 Samuel 7. After the repressive rule of Solomon, David's son, the nation split into two realms, each with its own line of kings.

   Jesus taught: Jesus was descended from David. In Jesus, the Davidic dynasty is restored, radically reinterpreted, and will continue forever. Jesus' kingship was very different in style from David's, John 18:36. David's life was marked by brutality and immorality. Jesus walked the way of a servant without limit, and calls His people to walk the same way. Jesus is, remarkably, the first of the New People of God, and at the same time, the King of that People. He is King and Servant in one Person.

   Jerusalem skyline: David captured Jerusalem, made it his capital, and called it the City of David, 2 Samuel 5:6–10. Eventually, David brought the Ark of the Covenant to Jerusalem, 2 Samuel 6. As time went by, David's name became inseparably linked to Jerusalem, Isaiah 37:16,35.

   Jesus taught: Christians are to look for the heavenly Jerusalem that they will enter when this life is done, Revelation ch. 21.

8. *Solomon's Temple*: After Solomon built the Temple, he placed the Ark of the Covenant into the Holy of Holies within it. The Babylonians destroyed Solomon's Temple in 587 B.C. The exiles who returned from Babylon built a replacement Temple and dedicated it in 515 B.C. Herod the Great

replaced this postexilic Temple with a grand and magnificent structure. It was begun in 19 B.C., took 82 years to build, and was destroyed by the Romans in A.D. 70.

Jesus taught: Jesus declared the Jerusalem Temple superseded and replaced, John 1:51, 2:13–22. Jesus is the cornerstone of the New Testament Temple, Ephesians 2:20. His people are "living stones" in that spiritual Temple, which is His walking, serving, "presence-of-God" community, 1 Peter 2:5. Though the religious leaders of His day hoped the nations would come to the Jerusalem Temple to worship the God of Israel there, Jesus sent His followers to the ends of the earth to proclaim His Person, forgiveness and mission.

9. *Altar*: The sacrificial system played an important role in the life of the nation. In 621 B.C., King Josiah carried out a great reform movement. The result was that the people could now offer sacrifice at only one place—the Jerusalem Temple. That meant that those who controlled the Temple, and its animal sellers and money changers, eventually became rich and powerful.

Jesus taught: Jesus attacked the religious leaders who controlled the Temple, and charged them with seeking power and money. Jesus fulfilled and superseded the sacrificial system when He sacrificed Himself for the sins of the world, once and for all. Paul tells us that God does not want His people to offer Him dead animals, but living bodies—living bodies to be used in service to God and others, Romans 12:1,2.

10. *Scroll*: After the exiles began returning from Babylon to Judah in 538 B.C., their scholars and teachers began collecting and studying their sacred scrolls.

Lamp, symbol for wisdom: Though some Jewish teachers referred to all their sacred writings as "wisdom," eventually some of the Old Testament books were specifically classified as wisdom writings. They said that the first thing God created was Wisdom (which many equated with the Pentateuch or Torah). They believed this was God's adviser in the process of creation.

Jesus taught: The written Word points beyond itself to the living Word, Jesus the Messiah. Jesus is the Bread of Life, the Light of the World, the Water of Life—terms that were used by Jewish rabbis to refer to their Old Testament writings. In Jesus, the Word finally became flesh, John 1:14; Hebrews 1:1–4. Jesus is the true wisdom, 1 Corinthians 1:24. More, Jesus is the Creator, John 1:1–4. Eternal life is to be found only in Jesus, John 5:39,40.

11. *Star of David superimposed on a map of the world*: Those who returned to Judea from exile in Babylon were called "Jews." As the centuries went by, and they remained under foreign control, many looked for a time when God would permit the Jews to rule the nations, just as other nations had ruled them, Daniel 7. Some thought that God would raise up a descendant of David to achieve this, Isaiah 9:1–7, 11:1–5.

Jesus taught: Jesus is the King of the universe, and those whom Jesus refers to as "the meek" share His lordship over creation, Matthew 5:5. Christians are to share Jesus' attitude toward the Father, the created order and other people. Jesus refused to focus on hopes that mattered most to the political and religious leaders of His day. He refused to spearhead a move to throw off Roman control and "re-establish" the Davidic Kingdom.

12. *Gravestone and skull*: During the centuries after the return from exile in Babylon, many Jews longed for the coming of the Messianic Age. Some of the rabbis taught that, when the Messianic Age came, the dead would rise from their graves to take part in it, Daniel 12:1–3.

Jesus taught: Christians do not dream about life in the land of Israel, but look forward to the day when Jesus will command the graves to give up the dead, John 5:28,29. On that day, Jesus will invite His people to enter His eternal home and will take care of them forever, Matthew 25:31–46.

B.   OTHER ISSUES IN THE GOSPELS

1.   The Relationship between the Risen Lord and the Spirit

At the top of frame 20 in the time line is a *dove*, the symbol for the Holy Spirit. The New Testament relates the risen Lord inseparably to the presence of the Holy Spirit. In John 14:16,18,23,26,28, Jesus assures His followers that He will come and remain among them. In Romans 8:9,10, Paul scarcely distinguishes between the risen Jesus and the Spirit. In 2 Corinthians 3:17, Paul refers to the Lord as the Spirit. Jesus continues among us in and through His Spirit. The Spirit continues the work of Jesus. Their work is one and inseparable.

The British theologian, F.F. Bruce, explains the matter as follows. After rising from the dead, Jesus pays His followers a number of "little visits" to assure them that He is still with and among them. In the ascension, He is saying, "Though there will be no more *visible* little visits, I am not going away. I shall remain among you *invisibly*." The point is that Jesus is still among us. In the ascension, Jesus did not *withdraw* His presence; He *transformed* it. Those who confess in the Apostles' creed that Jesus "sits at the right hand of God, the Father Almighty," should bear in mind that God does not have a right hand, and that the words refer to Jesus' *authority*, not to His *locality*. The point is that Jesus has been declared Lord of the Universe, and, as the God-Man, fills every corner of it. Furthermore, humanity either submits to Jesus as King of the universe and conforms to His servant-style, or it collapses.

2.   Second Coming? Or, Final Appearing?

The people of God form a family, a community of people, who live around the presence of Jesus—who is still among them as Savior and Lord. Strictly speaking, we now wait, not for Jesus' *Second Coming* (for He is among us continually), but for His *Final Appearing*. While we wait for that final, climactic event, we are to serve Him.

How are we to serve Him? Jesus assures us that He is all around us in disguise. He is the hungry one, the thirsty one, the stranger, the one lacking clothing, the sick one, the prisoner and so forth. As we serve those whom Jesus calls "the least of His brothers and sisters," we serve Him, Matthew 25:31–46.

Those who wait for Jesus' "final appearing" are to live *expectantly* (Matthew 25:1–13), *responsibly* (Matthew 25:14–30) and *compassionately*, Matthew 25:31–46.

3.   Conclusion

The basic issue of the New Testament is not: "Does God love us, and does God forgive us?" God does both, and has done so since creation and the fall into sin. True, the New Testament sees Jesus' death and resurrection as the final, climactic events through which the salvation of humanity is worked out, once and for all, 2 Corinthians 5:17–21. Even so, the key issue the New Testament raises is: "What kind of Messiah was Jesus? What was the nature of the Messianic Age that broke in with Him, and what does it imply for those who belong to His community?"

The answer is that Jesus came as a humble King who served. In grace and mercy, He calls His followers into His forgiving presence to teach them to do the same for each other. This is what Jesus' Messianic community is all about. In it, God's original intention for humanity (depicted in frame 2) is being restored.

Part 4

THE DIVINE PLAN IN MINIATURE

1. "In the beginning, God," Genesis 1:1. A *circle* is used as *the symbol for God*; as there is *one circle*, so there is *one God*. As a circle is *without beginning or end*, so God is without beginning or end—*eternal*. God always acts in *love*, and God's love goes *out* from God; this is depicted in frame 1 by arrows *going out from God*.

2. "Created the heavens and the earth," Genesis 1:1 (*sun, moon, stars, surface of the earth*). "Then God said, 'Let us make man,'" Genesis 1:26. "Male and female He created them," Genesis 1:27 (*male and female figures*). A good and loving God created a good universe and humanity to fulfill a divine plan and purpose. Humanity was *to know and praise God* (*raised hands*); in this, the concern was not God's ego, but humanity's happiness.

3. "In our image, after our likeness," Genesis 1:26 (*people serve God and each other; arrows go out from each person to God and neighbor, denoting servanthood in community*). God wanted humanity's behavior pattern to reflect God's behavior pattern: *love flowing out from self*.

4. Humanity sinned (*people no longer serve God and others, but themselves*). Death is the consequence of sin (*tombstone and skull*), Romans 5:12, 6:23.

5. People changed; God did not. God united the Godhead with humanity in the God-Man, Jesus the Messiah. Jesus lived the perfect servant life people were meant to live (but no longer can) for them.

6. Jesus suffered the death people deserve to die, and rose from the grave as Lord of life, death and eternity. Though death is still the *consequence* of sin, it is no longer the *punishment* for sin, Galatians 4:4,5.

7. God declares humanity forgiven through Jesus (*cross through the symbol for sin*), and invites and urges people to repent of what they are, and to trust in God's free and full forgiveness, won through Jesus' death on the cross. Jesus lives among His people through His Holy Spirit (*dove*) to teach them what He wants them to believe and do; the Holy Spirit uses the message of Jesus revealed in the Bible to do this. Jesus wants His people to try to live as God first intended humanity to live (*arrows to God and neighbor*). Their obedience is anything but perfect (*broken arrows*). Death is no longer an enemy to be feared, but a doorway into eternal life (*door with slats*). God's people know, and see in faith, what awaits them beyond death.

8. In the life to come (*cloud, denoting God's presence*), God will restore things to the way God first intended them to be. In eternity, God's people will live to praise God and serve each other. The divine plan will be restored. Throughout the sweep of God's saving plan, though people are never saved *by* servanthood, they are always saved *for* servanthood.

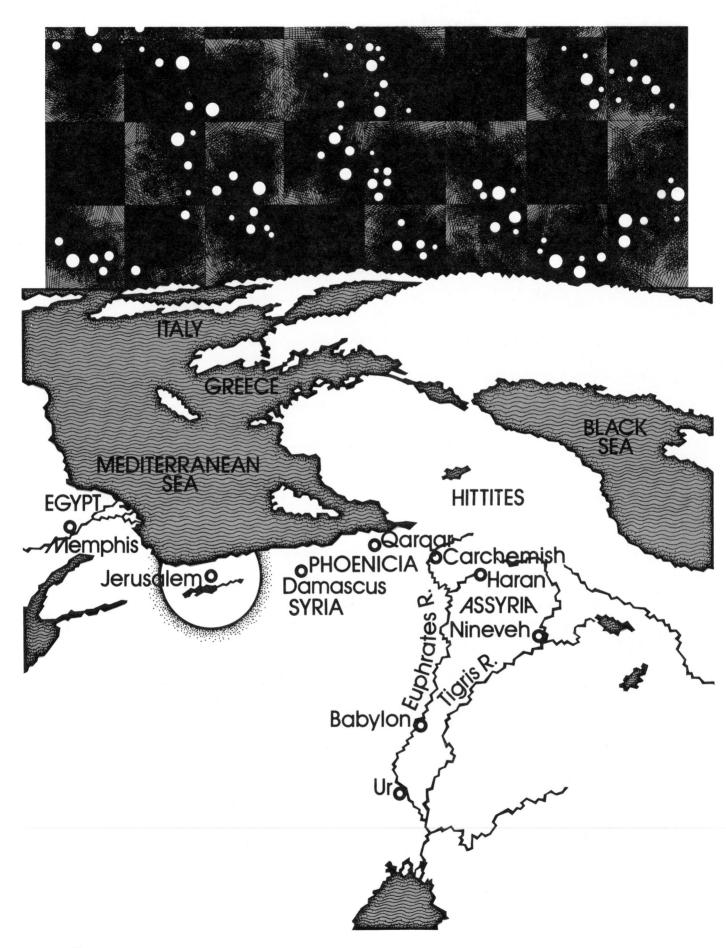

ITALY

GREECE

BLACK
SEA

MEDITERRANEAN
SEA

HITTITES

EGYPT

Memphis

Qarqar

PHOENICIA

Carchemish

Jerusalem

Damascus

Haran

SYRIA

ASSYRIA

Nineveh

Euphrates R.

Tigris R.

Babylon

Ur

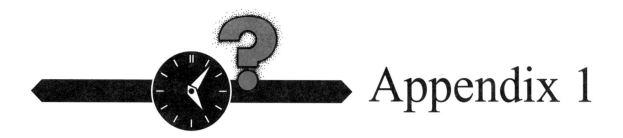

Appendix 1

THE *SECULAR* STORY BEHIND THE *BIBLICAL* STORY

When you take a Bible into your hands, you hold God's greatest gift to humanity. The Bible reveals God's heart and God's plan for the cosmos and humanity for time and eternity. It is, above all, the inspired record of God's dialogue with humanity. This inspired conversation did not take place while the original participants were sitting in comfortable chairs. It took place within the turmoil of history.

Though the dialogue relates to all creation and history, it took place within a rather tiny corner of the world—the region known today as the Middle East. Most of it took place within that land variously called Canaan, Israel and Palestine.

Israel stands at the eastern end of the Mediterranean Sea. Still today, Israel's location is important politically and geographically. In the world in which the biblical narrative unfolds, Israel's history was greatly affected by the power play that went on among its neighbors to the south, north, east and west.

The biblical writers read the events that constitute the biblical narrative while wearing "theological spectacles," so to say; what follows is a condensed account of how a secular historian might have reported the events behind the Old Testament narrative.

1. THE BIG POLITICAL PLAYERS: A SUMMARY

The ancient nation of Israel stood where three continents meet—Africa, Asia and Europe. To the south of Israel, in Africa, lies Egypt. When the biblical story begins, Egypt is already an old empire. As a succession of dynasties came and went, Egypt's political power and influence rose and fell.

Recent events in the world have made people today more familiar with names such as Syria, Iraq and Iran. These countries are located within or near the valleys of the Tigris and Euphrates rivers—a region traditionally referred to as "Mesopotamia." Mesopotamia is made up of two Greek words for "between the rivers." In biblical times, this region was controlled by a succession of empires: the Assyrian, Babylonian and Medo-Persian empires.

Later, and to the west, came the Greek and Roman empires. First, Alexander the Great and his successors conquered and controlled the eastern Mediterranean region and sought to impose Greek philosophy and culture on all they controlled. Later, the Romans swallowed up the Greek empire, took control of all regions around the Mediterranean rim, and expanded their empire to embrace the regions west of Rome.

2. CLOSER NEIGHBORS AND TROUBLEMAKERS

The Israelites who entered Canaan after the exodus from Egypt had to determine what to do with that land's original inhabitants, the Canaanites. They also had to deal with the Philistines, who settled along the Mediterranean coast and controlled the five cities of Gath, Gaza, Ashkelon, Ashdod and Ekron. They had to deal with the Arameans (Syrians), whose capital city was Damascus. And they had to deal with other lesser tribes and kingdoms located around their borders, namely, the Ammonites, Moabites, Edomites, Ishmaelites, Midianites and Amalekites—most of whom were related to them.

3.   THE EGYPTIAN CONNECTION

During the period 1550–1200 B.C., Egypt claimed control over Syria and Palestine. However, these claims were often contested by the Hittites and the Mitanni peoples of eastern Asia Minor. By 1,200 B.C., Egyptian control of Palestine was more theory than fact, and numerous groups from within and without Palestine were fighting to control various parts of it. The resulting instability took its toll on the region's trade and economy. The Amarna letters, written during the reigns of the Egyptian pharaohs Amenhotep III and IV (ca.1403–1347 B.C.), allude to the events of this period.

The book of Exodus describes God's rescue of Jacob's descendants from Egypt as the key event in their history. The Israelites continued to remember Egypt as the land of bondage from which God rescued them with "signs and wonders," Deuteronomy 26:8. (Centuries later, a small group of fugitives from Judah feared Babylonian wrath and fled back to Egypt, taking the prophet Jeremiah with them, Jeremiah chs. 42–44. To return to Egypt was to undo the Exodus!)

4.   IN THE LAND

The book of Joshua describes the Israelite conquest of Palestine. The book of Judges describes, among other things, the three major problems the new residents in Palestine faced: political disunity, spiritual syncretism (a mixing of beliefs and practices) and dynastic uncertainty. The opening chapters of First Samuel describe how the Israelites eventually came to have kings—the first of whom was Saul. However, by the time of Saul's death, the Philistines and the Ammonites seemed to control much of the land. The writer of 1 Samuel 13:19–22 states that the Israelites had to look to the Philistines to supply them with weapons of war and tools for agriculture.

Indications are that King David (Saul's successor) managed to deal with the Philistine threat. Under David and his successor, Solomon, Israel became the dominant power in the region and experienced its golden age. But when Solomon died, the previously United Kingdom split into two small kingdoms: Israel to the north and Judah to the south.

To complicate matters, about five years after Solomon's death, Pharaoh Shishak I of Egypt sought to reassert Egyptian control over the regions to his north, and plundered Israel and Judah, and Jerusalem and its Temple, 1 Kings 14:25–28. However, the Egyptians were not able to maintain tight control over Judah and Israel, and played only a sporadic role in the power struggles of the next several centuries.

As Egypt waned, nations to the north, east and west of Israel continued to cast covetous eyes on Egypt. Little wonder, because Egypt, with its remarkably fertile and productive Nile Valley, was the breadbasket of the ancient world. However, nations such as those in Mesopotamia could not travel "as the crow flies" to Egypt because of the deserts in between. Travel across desert regions became possible only with the domestication of the camel, and even then, no nation could provide every member of its army with a personal "ship of the desert." Armies travelled by foot. So, as nation after nation strove to gain control of Egypt, they marched through—and annexed—Israel, for Israel lay on the land-bridge between Egypt to the south and its covetous competitors to the north.

5.   SYRIA AND PHOENICIA: SQUABBLES AND ALLIANCES

Israel and Judah's close neighbors, Syria and Phoenicia, were also subject to threats from the armies of powerful empires. Yet these nations squabbled among themselves as well. The Old Testament tells us that Israel, Syria and Phoenicia were each striving to become the dominant force in the region. Commerce and control of trade routes were motivating forces. It was to Phoenicia's benefit to try to maintain good relations with Israel and Syria. Phoenicia's economy was based on seafaring trade among Mediterranean nations, and its traders needed goods produced by Israel and Syria. Furthermore, goods from more distant countries had to pass through Israel and Syria to reach Phoenician ships.

Some of the rulers of Phoenicia, Syria and Israel used treaties and marriages to forge political alliances. For example, during the reigns of Omri of Israel and his successor and son Ahab, relations between Israel and Syria were strained. At the same time, relations between Israel and Phoenicia were good, and were sealed by the marriage of Jezebel, the daughter of the king of the Phoenician city of Sidon, and Ahab, king of Israel, 1 Kings 16:31. This in turn led to something of a marriage between Phoenicia and Israel's cultural and religious traditions. It also gave the affluent in Israel opportunity to gain access to Phoenician luxuries such as ivory furnishings, Amos 6:4. (Jerusalem, Judah's capital, revealed Phoenician influence, too; its temple was designed by Phoenician architects using a Phoenician pattern.)

6.   ASSYRIA

With the gradual weakening of Egyptian influence, the Neo-Assyrian empire in Mesopotamia increased in power and influence, and soon became the influential factor in the histories of Israel and Judah and those of other regions between Assyria and Egypt, such as Syria and Phoenicia. To deal with the threat, several states in the region of Syria and Israel joined forces in an effort to stem the Assyrian advance into their territory. In 853 B.C., the opposing sides locked horns at Qarqar. King Ahab of Israel was said to have sent 2,000 chariots and 10,000 foot soldiers to battle. The coalition of smaller states came out the apparent winner. However, because necessity had been the mother of cooperation in the battle of Qarqar, relations among these small states remained anything but harmonious.

Though Judah took no part in the encounter at Qarqar, it could not isolate itself entirely from foreign influence and the power struggles that were taking place in the region. Judah sought to pursue a policy of isolationism, but such a policy was impossible. In 735 B.C., Syria and Israel joined forces in an attempt to force Ahaz of Judah to join them in a coalition designed to stem Assyrian incursions into the area.

In seeking to secure itself within Mesopotamia, Assyria set out to establish buffer regions around its borders, and to control Egypt to obtain a sure source of food for its armies. In 721 B.C., Assyria swallowed up Israel and led its people into exile and oblivion; Judah was made a vassal state, was forced to pay an annual tribute and was forced to support Assyrian military undertakings in the region.

Egypt, being well aware of Assyria's ambitions, set out to make the small states to its immediate north a buffer between itself and Assyria. To achieve its goal, Egypt made numerous promises to its small northern neighbors, but rarely kept them. Isaiah referred to Egypt as a broken cane that offered little support to those who leaned on it; Egypt was, in fact, dangerous, Isaiah 36:6.

While all this was going on, prophets such as Amos, Hosea, Isaiah and Micah watched, thought and taught. Though politically they sensed what Assyrian ambitions would eventually mean for Israel and Judah, what they said and wrote went beyond political opinion to spiritual diagnosis. They interpreted what they saw in theological terms. They understood clearly that there is no such thing as a purely political, secular event.

7.   BABYLON

Though Assyria gained control of Egypt in the middle of the 7th century B.C., Assyria overextended itself in doing so, found it could not maintain its military machine, and finally lost its grip on Egypt, 2 Kings 23:29–35. With Assyria's demise, another player walked on to the stage of history—Babylon! Egypt immediately saw the emerging Babylon as a threat, with the result that, in 609 B.C., Pharaoh Neco of

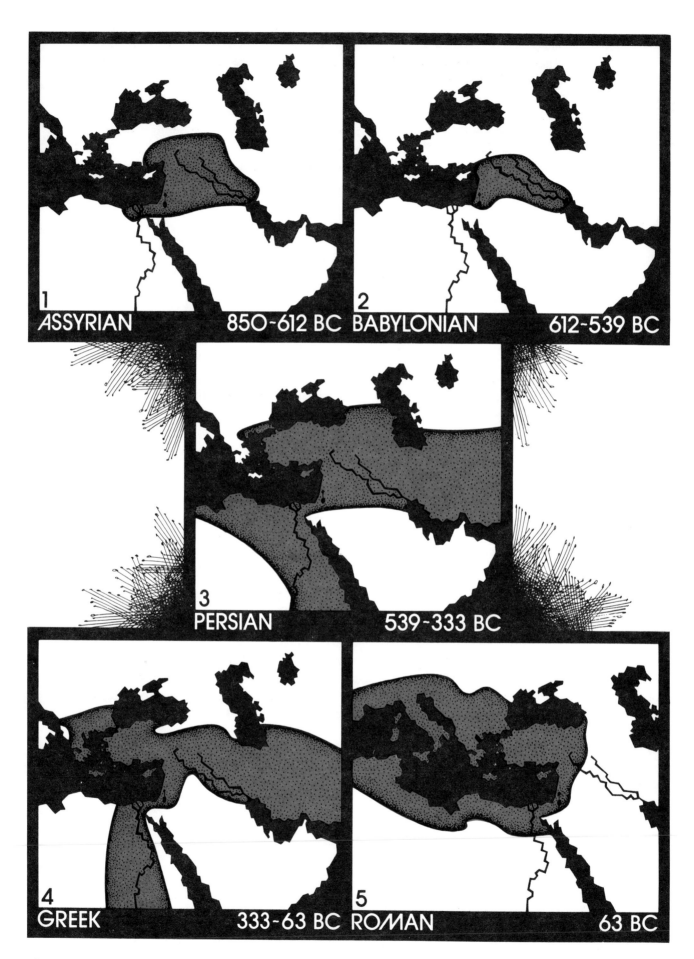

1 ASSYRIAN 850-612 BC

2 BABYLONIAN 612-539 BC

3 PERSIAN 539-333 BC

4 GREEK 333-63 BC

5 ROMAN 63 BC

Egypt led his armies north in an attempt to prop up a dying Assyria. Though Neco's efforts were short-lived and unsuccessful, they drastically changed the history of Judah. Because Judah felt it had suffered long enough under the Assyrian heel, more than anything else it wanted Babylon to deliver the final thrust to a dying Assyria. Therefore, King Josiah of Judah, in an effort to stem Neco's advance, led his army into battle against the Egyptians. In the ensuing battle at Megiddo, the Egyptians proved the victors, and Josiah lost his life, 2 Kings 23:28–30.

The kings of Judah who succeeded Josiah (two sons, a grandson and then another son) sought to secure their throne and borders by playing off one neighboring power against the other. They failed, and brought about the collapse of Judah in the process. After King Jehoiakim (Josiah's son) revolted in 601 B.C., King Nebuchadnezzar of Babylon marched around the Fertile Crescent and put the revolt down. Jehoiakim died three months before Jerusalem's fall in 597 B.C. His son Jehoiachin, who replaced him, surrendered immediately, and, together with thousands of others, was taken into exile in Babylon. Another son of Josiah, Zedekiah, was made a puppet king, replacing Jehoiachin. When he, too, revolted in 589 B.C., Nebuchadnezzar stormed around the Fertile Crescent, devastated Judah, sacked and destroyed Jerusalem and its Temple, killed many of its political and religious leaders, including Zedekiah's sons, and again took thousands into exile, including Zedekiah whom he had blinded.

The Babylonians, like the Assyrians before them, set out to control subject peoples through fear, and destroy national identities and religious allegiances by removing those they conquered from their nation-state, and assimilating them with other captive ethnic groups.

In the ancient biblical world, many believed that when a nation died, its deity had died—or was showing impotence or lack of concern for its people. In contrast, many who experienced the exile in Babylon came to understand that their God was not confined to any particular territory, nor was their God limited in power. There were other ways of explaining their presence as exiles in Babylon. And so, though Psalm 137:4 contains the cry of a people recently removed from their national state and national shrine, many came to see that they could worship and serve God even while living in lands other than Judah. This learning process was made easier by the overthrow of Babylon by Cyrus the Persian in 539 B.C.

8.   ENTER PERSIA

In 539 B.C., Babylonian power gave way to Persian power when Cyrus the Persian and his successors carved out a kingdom that stretched from India to Ethiopia. Cyrus saw his capture of Babylon as a grant of Marduk, the chief god of Babylon, who declared him the legitimate king of the city. The city had, in fact, been handed over to Cyrus by Babylonian priests who were disenchanted with Nabonidus, the last of the Babylonian kings. The priests were angered since Nabonidus had deserted Babylon to reside in north-west Arabia. In addition, he made his son, Belshazzar, regent in Babylon, and for ten years, he had not attended the annual New Year Festival for the enthronement of Marduk in Babylon. Even Isaiah spoke of Cyrus as God's "messiah," 44:28–45:1.

Cyrus pursued an enlightened policy. He permitted foreign exiles within his realm to return to their homelands and reestablish their religious practices—as long as the move did not interfere with the peace

The illustration depicts Israel's position in relation to the geography and expansionist policies of surrounding nations. The five maps on the facing page depict the empires that played a key role in the history of Israel. The grip that the first four empires managed to keep on Israel (whether northern Israel or southern Judah) was sometimes tight and harsh, and at other times loose and patronizing. The illustration does not depict the part Egypt played in Israel's fortunes, and the nuisance value that Syria became to Israel on numerous occasions.

and stability of the empire. However, though many exiles returned to Judah, they were not permitted to establish themselves as an independent nation, but remained part of the Persian *satrapy* (province) known as "Beyond the River."

Those who returned to Judah became known as "Jews," and developed the system of belief that today is known as "Judaism." Though they were grateful for the rights and privileges they enjoyed under the Persians, they experienced some agony. King Jehoiachin, who had been taken to Babylon in 597 B.C., had still been alive in 560 B.C., 2 Kings 25:27–30. Many hoped that when the period of exile in Babylon ended, Jehoiachin would return to Jerusalem with them to reestablish the Davidic dynasty and kingdom. Their hopes were not fulfilled; Jehoiachin did not survive long enough to join the exiles who returned to Judah. He died in Babylon some time after 560 B.C. The result was that those who eventually returned to reestablish themselves in Judah and Jerusalem felt that, though God had rescued them from Babylon, two things were wrong. *First*, they remained under foreign control. *Second*, the Davidic dynasty had apparently come to an end. Despite these frustrations, for several hundred years the Jews enjoyed a period of peace and stability they had not known for centuries.

Though many of the exiles continued to live beyond the borders of Judah, and though many rose to high rank—Esther and Mordecai, for example—many others deliberately developed a lifestyle that would set them apart from those non-Jews among whom they lived. Increasing importance was placed on Sabbath observances, circumcision, food laws and Passover observance within the family context.

9. ENTER GREECE

During the Persian period, the Jews had been able to preserve their religious identity without too much difficulty. But in 331 B.C., the Persian Empire fell to that of Alexander the Great of Macedon. He was 20 years old when he came to power; his father had been assassinated. With the advent of Greek control, Alexander and his successors sought to impose Hellenism (Greek philosophy, language and way of life) on all within the borders of their empire.

Upon Alexander's death in 323 B.C., the Greek Empire was divided into three parts. One general, Ptolemy, gained control of Egypt. A second general, Seleucus, ruled the Mesopotamian region and, for a time, his territories extended to the borders of India. A third section, centering around Greece itself, was torn by wars of succession until the Romans assumed control of the region in the second century B.C.

To complicate matters, Judah found itself caught up in a tug-of-war between the Ptolemies who ruled Egypt, and the Seleucids who ruled Syria and the territories to the east. The Ptolemies eventually managed to gain control over Judah, and retained that control until 198 B.C. when the Seleucids took over.

Though the returning exiles had rebuilt the Jerusalem Temple and rededicated it in 515 B.C., and though Jews scattered beyond the borders of Judah (*diaspora* Jews) felt a strong attachment to that sacred edifice, few of them could visit it. Furthermore, though many diaspora Jews supported the financial needs of the Temple, the family circle and the synagogue served as the focal points for community life in the regions beyond Judah's borders.

Though the Greeks did not at first use force to impose Hellenism on subject peoples, they let it be known that their traditions and way of life were superior. The temples, gymnasiums and theaters they built to serve their own needs appealed strongly to many among their subject peoples, including some of the more youthful Jews and the Jewish upper class. Many Jews learned to speak Greek. The time came when many Jews could speak *only* Greek—with the result that during the last centuries B.C., the Jews in Alexandria translated their sacred writings into Greek. They added several other Greek texts (today referred to as the Apocrypha) to the Hebrew texts they translated. The final collection became known as the Septuagint.

As time went by, an increasing number of Jews adopted Greek dress and customs, took part in Greek games, and studied Greek philosophy. Some went so far as to blend Hellenism with Judaism. Some ignored Jewish dietary requirements. Some aspiring Jewish male athletes sought to have the marks of circumcision reversed surgically. Some applauded these moves. Others were appalled by them.

In 168 B.C., the Seleucid, Antiochus IV Epiphanes, set out to eliminate Judaism and replace it with Hellenism. He sought to do away with Sabbath observance, circumcision, dietary practices and the possession of the Torah. To cap it all off, he tried to enforce the worship of Greek gods—and even of himself as the incarnation of the deity. Some Jews readily conformed to his dictates. Others conformed merely to save their lives. Some withdrew into hiding to practice their Jewish ways. Others suffered martyrdom, 2 Maccabees chs. 6,7.

The breaking point came when Antiochus IV ordered Jews to offer pagan sacrifices. In 167 B.C., some Jews under the leadership of the Maccabees (a Jewish priestly family) revolted—and managed to remove the Seleucid yoke from their necks. Though Antiochus had desecrated the Temple in 168 B.C., the Maccabees purified and rededicated it in 165 B.C.—an event the Jews continue to celebrate annually at Hanukkah. Then, from about 165 to 63 B.C., the Jews enjoyed a measure of political freedom under the rule, first of the Maccabees, and then of their descendants and successors, the Hasmoneans.

Even so, all was not well within the realm. First, the Seleucids had been ready to strike a deal with the Maccabees because they were aware of the growing might of Rome. Second, the Jews soon realized that though they had won the war against the Seleucids, they had lost the peace—for the Hasmoneans who ruled them did so more in the manner of Greek princes than Jewish leaders.

10. FINALLY, ROME

During the first century B.C., Rome began to make its presence felt more and more around the Mediterranean basin. In 63 B.C., the Roman general Pompey took control of Judea (a postexilic term for Judah). The Romans took advantage of a bitter rivalry between two Hasmoneans, Hyrcanus II, who had succeeded to the throne in 67 B.C., and his brother, the vicious Aristobulus. The Romans chose the weaker brother, Hyrcanus, as their representative; Pompey named him High Priest.

Hyrcanus' chief minister was his close friend, Antipater, from the province of Idumea, the territory of Edom. Antipater was politically shrewd. He earned gratitude from Julius Caesar for his loyalty. Among his rewards were powerful positions for his sons, Herod and Phasael. Herod, too, proved his loyalty to Rome and was nominated by the Roman senate to be king of Judea in 40 B.C. He was not able to succeed to his position until 37 B.C. since the Parthian empire had invaded and claimed Judea in the meantime; Herod had to reconquer the territory with Roman help.

After Herod's death in 4 B.C., the Romans appointed his son Archelaeus as ethnarch ("ruler of the people") of Judea and Samaria, but deposed him in A.D. 6. After that time, except for one brief period, Judea was governed by Roman officials known as procurators, few of whom were sensitive enough to govern the unusual people they were sent to govern. The name of one of those procurators remains prominent in history: Pontius Pilate.

In Matthew 2:1, we read, "In the time of King Herod, after Jesus was born in Bethlehem of Judah...." In Matthew 27:26, we read, "After flogging Jesus, Pilate handed him over to be crucified."

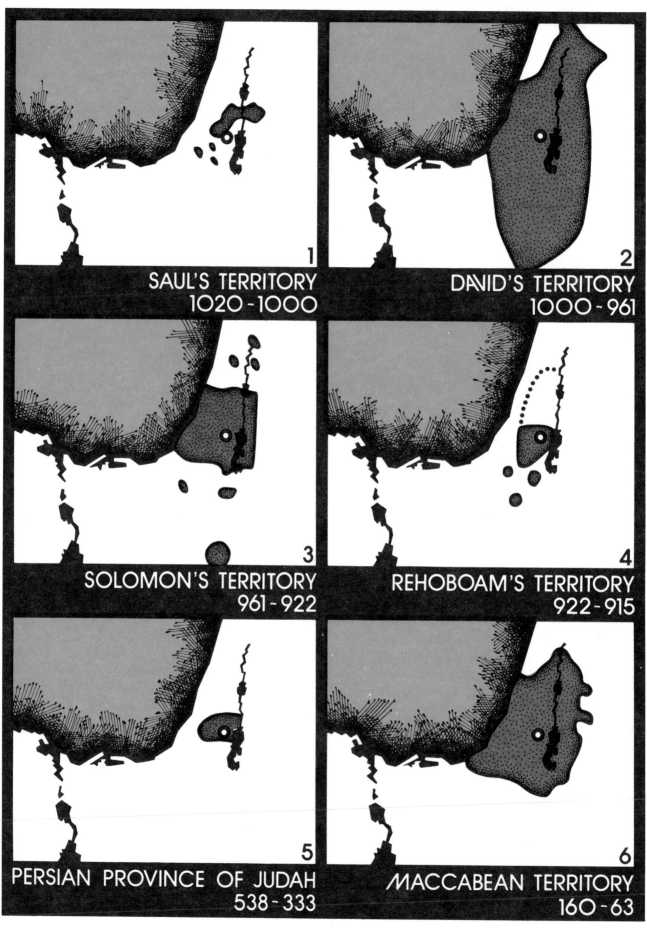

1

SAUL'S TERRITORY
1020-1000

2

DAVID'S TERRITORY
1000-961

3

SOLOMON'S TERRITORY
961-922

4

REHOBOAM'S TERRITORY
922-915

5

PERSIAN PROVINCE OF JUDAH
538-333

6

MACCABEAN TERRITORY
160-63

11. SUMMARY: MEMORIES AND DREAMS

The illustration shows how Israel's borders increased and decreased as the nation's fortunes waxed and waned.

1. The size of the territory Saul ruled is uncertain. See 1 Samuel 14:47,48.

2. David's realm was large. He was made king over Judah at Hebron about 1000 B.C., and about seven years later was proclaimed king over the Northern Kingdom of Israel as well. He conducted successful campaigns against the neighboring Philistines, Moabites, Arameans (Syrians), Ammonites, Edomites and Amalekites; note Genesis 15:18–20. Under him Israel became a nation of some importance in the ancient Near East.

3. Though Solomon inherited David's realm, he eventually lost territory in both the south and north, 1 Kings 11:14–25.

4. After Solomon's death, the one kingdom split into two kingdoms—Israel to the north and Judah to the south. Rehoboam succeeded his father, Solomon, in the south. Jeroboam was proclaimed king of the Northern Kingdom, Israel. The history of Israel came to an end in 721 B.C. The Babylonians devastated Judah in 587 B.C. and took thousands of its leading citizens into exile.

5. The Persians overthrew Babylon in 539 B.C., and permitted exiled peoples to return to their homelands. However, the Jews were not granted political freedom; Judah became part of the Persian *satrapy* (or province) known as "Beyond the River."

6. The Greeks destroyed Persian power in 331 B.C. After Alexander the Great's death in 323 B.C., the empire was divided among his generals. The Ptolemies ruled Judah (from Egypt) until 198 B.C. The Seleucids ruled Judah (from Syria) until 160 B.C., when Jewish forces under the Maccabees gained independence for the Jews. Frame 6 shows the approximate extent of the Maccabean Kingdom after John Hyrcanus became ruler and high priest in 134 B.C.

THE GRAND FINALE—JESUS' KINGDOM

1. Some believe that the central issue at stake in the Gospels and in the whole of the New Testament is that, in Jesus, the long-expected Savior finally came, died for the sins of the world, rose from the grave, and ascended to prepare a place for those who believe in Him. These truths indeed are central to the teaching of the New Testament. However, more is at stake.

2. The central issue at stake in the Gospels is the nature of Jesus' kingship. At His baptism, Jesus was declared to be King ("You are my Son, the Beloved," Mark 1:11; see Psalm 2:7) and Servant ("With you I am well pleased," Mark 1:1; see Isaiah 42:1). The point is: The Jewish people were waiting for a Messiah who would restore the long-defunct Davidic dynasty, reestablish the Davidic kingdom, gain freedom from Roman control and establish political independence. Instead, they got a King who walked the way of a servant-without-limit, sought the company of those considered nobodies and outcasts, and washed the disciples' feet.

   The Jewish people were expecting someone to rescue them from foreign domination, not a Servant-Messiah. As George McDonald once wrote:

   > They were all waiting for a king
   >   To slay their foes and raise them high;
   > Thou cam'st a little baby thing
   >   that made a woman cry.

   To which might be added two lines:

   > Thou cam'st to do Thy servant thing,
   >   On cruel cross to die!

3. In Mark's Gospel, Jesus predicts His coming passion and death three times, 8:31; 9:30–32; 10:32–34. Each time, the disciples respond in a way that reveals they have no idea what He is talking about. After the first prediction, Peter protests. After the second, the disciples ask Jesus who will be His "prime minister" in the kingdom that they believe He is about to establish. After the third, James and John ask that they might sit to His right and left when He is enthroned.

4. The illustration shows the nature of the kingdom Jesus came to establish. Though it reflects Jesus washing the disciples' feet in the Upper Room as described in John 13:1–17, it describes the foundational issue at stake in each Gospel. At lower right, Jesus washes Peter's feet—who, in turn, appears awkward and embarrassed, for surely the Messiah does not perform tasks traditionally allocated to slaves! Jesus is then shown at center as King (*crown*) and Servant. At right are symbols of the crucified Jesus and the empty tomb; when Jesus' Father raised His Son from the dead, He endorsed the nature of Jesus' Messiahship. The members of Jesus' new community are shown in stylized form around Him. Naturally they are called to do more than hold hands; they are called to serve Jesus by serving each other and the world around them. The Risen Jesus continues among His followers today in and through His Holy Spirit (*dove*).

   In short, the entire New Testament points beyond itself to God's Word-in-Flesh, a strange King who washes feet and summons His community to do the same.

Appendix 2

KEY OLD TESTAMENT NARRATIVES: SAUL, DAVID, SOLOMON AND JOSIAH

Preliminary comments

1. To understand the Old Testament narrative, it is important to be familiar with the details of the reigns of Saul, David, Solomon and Josiah. The reign of Josiah is of considerable importance, for it was during his reign that, in 621 B.C., worship was finally centralized in Jerusalem.

2. The narrative outlining Israelite history was completed in Babylon, 2 Kings 25:27–30. It is possible that an earlier edition of the work was completed during the reign of Josiah, 2 Kings 23:25. This "earlier" edition reflects optimism, for it presents Josiah as one who restored the Davidic Kingdom in that Josiah, a descendant of David, ruled Judah and Israel from Jerusalem, and centralized all worship in the Jerusalem Temple, 2 Kings chs. 22,23.

   The "later" edition, completed in Babylon, grieves over the fact that the people of God are in exile in Babylon. It struggles with questions such as: "Why are we here? Where did we go wrong? Will we ever go back? Will the Davidic dynasty ever be restored?" It finds hope in the fact that Jehoiachin, taken to Babylon in 597 B.C. at the age of 18, is still alive in 560 B.C.—and since he is only 55 years of age, there is a chance that he will live through the exile, return to Jerusalem, and restore the Davidic dynasty.

3. In the Old Testament, the spirit of God raises up, and/or comes on, the judges Othniel, Gideon, Jephthah and Samson—then King Saul (1 Samuel 10:6–13; 19:23,24) and King David, 1 Samuel 16:13; note 16:14,15. After David, the next king on whom the spirit of God comes is Jesus. However, during the intervening period the spirit of God comes on the prophets—who tell the kings they are to live under God's covenant and rule according to it.

A.   Prior to Saul

1. The central theme of 1 Samuel 1:1–7:2 is how the Ark of the Covenant got from the shrine at Shiloh (Ephraim) to Kiriath-jearim. It caused considerable discomfort to the Philistines along the way, who had captured it from Israel. They returned it on a cart hauled by cows. Some years later, David got it from Kiriath-jearim and placed it in a tent he built for it in Jerusalem, 2 Samuel 6: note especially verse 17. The nature of the shrine in Shiloh is uncertain, 1 Samuel 1:9,24; 2:22; 3:3,15. Though the Ark of the Covenant was deposited in Kiriath-jearim (1 Samuel 7:2), it turned up in other places during Samuel's time (1 Samuel 10:17) and also during Saul's reign, 1 Samuel 14:18; 21:1–6. See also Judges 20:26–28.

2. More narrowly, 1 Samuel chs. 1–3 tell us about the birth of Samuel, (a Levite according to 1 Chronicles 6:33ff), the demise of the priest Eli's family, the eventual loss of favor by the priest Abiathar (1 Samuel 2:33; see also 1 Kings 2:26,27), and the rise to power of Zadok, 1 Samuel 2:35,36; see also 1 Kings 2:35.

3. Both Eli's sons (1 Samuel 2:12–17,22) and Samuel's sons (1 Samuel 8:1–3) were unfit to succeed their respective fathers in office. Hence, the issue that needed to be determined was that of succession and the form of government. Finally, Saul was appointed king, Samuel chs. 8–11.

4. The appointment of a ruler is outlined in 1 Samuel chs. 8–12. The terms "king" and "prince" (RSV translation) weave their way through the narratives in this section. The term prince is always positive, for God is still the king of the people and the prince is merely God's earthly representative. The term king can be viewed in a good sense, but whenever the future ruler is thought of negatively, the term *king* (not *prince*) is used. Solomon appears to be the villain in 1 Samuel 8:10–18.

B.   Saul (1 Samuel)

1. Saul himself is never referred to negatively in 1 Samuel 8–11. However, Samuel fired Saul from office on two occasions. In ch. 13, Saul interfered in the duties of a priest (see 10:8) and, in ch. 15, failed to eliminate all Israel's enemies in a "holy war."

2. The term "a man after God's own heart" first appears in 1 Samuel 13:14. The narrative that follows reveals that the term implies, "David worshiped *one God in one city, Jerusalem.*"

3. In ch. 14, though Saul's son Jonathan betrays skill as a soldier in battle, no reference is made to him consulting or praying to God prior to fighting the Philistines. Perhaps the suggestion is that David is a more appropriate candidate to succeed Saul.

4. In 1 Samuel 16, David is enlisted into Saul's service as a musician and armor-bearer.

5. 1 Samuel tells several other stories about how David first entered Saul's service, 17:17ff, 17:31ff, 17:55ff. Though 1 Samuel 17 states that David killed Goliath, 2 Samuel 21:19 ascribes the achievement to Elhanan; but see also 1 Chronicles 20:5.

6. In 1 Samuel 18:1–4, Jonathan gives David tokens suggesting he knows (and accepts!) that David will be the next king.

7. Saul tries to pin David to the wall with a spear, 18:10,11.

8. Saul gives David his second daughter (Michal) rather than the first (Merab), 18:17–29.

9. In 1 Samuel 19, David and Jonathan have the first of a number of amicable conversations.

10. Saul tries to pin David to the wall a second time, 19:8–10.

11. David flees from Michal (and Saul), possibly on their wedding night, 19:11–17.

12. David goes to Ramah and Saul pursues him, 19:18–24.

13. The spirit of God comes on Saul a second time, 19:23,24; see 10:6–13.

14. Jonathan talks to David, and Saul tries to kill Jonathan, ch. 20; note 20:14–17.

15. David gets food and Goliath's sword from the priests at Nob, ch. 21:1–9.

16. David tries to become a vassal of the Philistines, 21:10–15.

17. David gathers a band of supporters, 22:1,2.

18. For security reasons, David places his parents in Moab, 22:3–5. (Note: Ruth was a Moabitess.)

19. Saul kills the priests at Nob, 22:6–23.

20. David defends the people of Keilah, ch. 23. He hopes they will offer him sanctuary, but flees when he suspects they will hand him over to Saul.

21. David has an opportunity to kill Saul, but does not do so, ch. 24. Note 24:20,21.

22. David runs a "protection business," ch. 25.

23. David gets some new wives (Abigail and Ahinoam), and loses Michal (Saul's daughter), 25:39–44.

24. Once again, David could have killed Saul, ch. 26. Some significant Holy Land theology occurs in 1 Samuel 26:20. David feared that he might have to live permanently beyond the borders of Judah where he would be forced to serve other gods—and feared that he might die there, "away from the presence of the Lord." He suggests that God lives only in *Israel*.

25. David becomes a Philistine vassal, 27:1–7. Achish of Gath gives him Ziklag.

26. David annihilates the Amalekites, and lies to the Philistines, 27:8–12.

27. Saul consults the witch at Endor, ch. 28. She predicts his approaching death.

28. Note the tension: Will David be forced to fight against his own people, ch. 29? After David is "off the hook," he finds Ziklag plundered, ch. 30. David's people contemplate killing him, but he saves the situation, 30:6.

29. David sends presents to the clan leaders of Judah, 30:26–31. It is, after all, "election year," for Saul is about to be eliminated.

30. Saul and his army are defeated at the battle of Gilboa. Three of Saul's sons are killed, 31:2. Saul commits suicide, and is eventually buried by the men of Jabesh-gilead, 31:4,11–13. (Note: For Jabesh-gilead, see Judges 19–21 and 1 Samuel 11; also 2 Samuel 2:4b–7. Furthermore, 1 Chronicles 10:6 states that the Philistines wiped out Saul's entire family, thus saving David the task of having to do so, 2 Samuel 21.)

C.   David

Jonathan had extracted from David the promise that, when David became king, he would not annihilate Jonathan's family, 1 Samuel 20:12–17. David made a similar promise to Saul, 1 Samuel 24:16–22. Abigail eventually vindicated what David did to his opponents, 1 Samuel 25:23–31, especially vv. 29–31.

In fitting together the Saul/David narrative, it is helpful to remember that Abner, Saul's general, was Saul's cousin, 1 Samuel 14:50. Joab, David's general, was David's nephew and Solomon's cousin, as was Amasa whom David's son Absalom chose to be his general; see 2 Samuel 17:25, and note that Zeruiah was David's sister. Joab eventually killed both Abner and Amasa, and on his deathbed David instructed Solomon to have Joab done to death.

1. David laments for Saul and Jonathan, 2 Samuel ch. 1. He is then made king of Judah at Hebron, 2:1–4a.

2. The Northern Kingdom does not want David for its king, 2:4b–7. Abner, Saul's cousin and general, makes Saul's son, Ishbosheth, king of the North, 2:8–11.

3. A brutal contest is staged between the Northerners and Judah, 2:12–32. Eventually Abner kills Asahel, David's nephew, a brother of Joab (David's nephew and general). There is a long war between Judah and Israel, 3:1.

4. David obtains more "Hebron" wives and concubines, 3:2–5.

5. Abner apparently hopes and tries to make himself king of the North, 3:6–11, but fails in the attempt. He schemes with David to have David gain control of the North, 3:12–21.

6. Joab kills Abner. After all, if there is to be one realm, there is room for only one general, 3:22–39. The Northern king is beheaded; David has his executioners brutally killed, ch. 4.

7. David gains control over the Northern realm, 5:1–5.

8. David captures Jerusalem, 5:6–10; he has the blind and lame within the city killed (see Matthew 21:14).

9. David builds himself a palace, 5:11,12.

10. David obtains more "Jerusalem" wives and concubines, 5:13–16; note that Solomon was born in Jerusalem.

11. David subdues the Philistines, 5:17–25; they eventually form his bodyguard, 15:18.

12. David brings the Ark of the Covenant to Jerusalem, ch. 6, and puts it into a tent. David's first wife (Michal, Saul's daughter), is dismissed from his favor and bedroom. See 1 Samuel 18:20–27; 25:44; 2 Samuel 3:12–16; 6:16, 20–23.

13. David decides to build God a "house," a Temple, ch. 7. God says He does not want a Temple, 7:4–7. He will, however, make a "house," a dynasty, out of David (7:8–17) that will last "forever," 7:13,16,29. David thanks God for the dynasty, but does not refer to the Temple while doing so, 7:18–29.

14. David expands his kingdom—brutally, 2 Samuel chs. 8 and 10.

15. David "shows kindness" to Jonathan's son, Mephibosheth, ch. 9. It is possible that he placed him under house arrest. Some believe, with good reason, that ch. 9 should follow ch. 21.

16. David seduces Bathsheba, chs. 11,12. This action involved adultery, murder and the breaking of "holy war" laws that said: During war, "no sex," Deuteronomy 20.

17. David's son, Amnon, rapes his half-sister Tamar, 13:1–19.

18. Absalom, Amnon's half-brother and Tamar's brother, has Amnon killed, 13:20–33. Absalom flees to his maternal grandfather, Talmai, king of Geshur, 13:34–39.

19. Joab arranges for Absalom to return to Jerusalem—and to the family circle, ch. 14.

20. Absalom begins casting doubt on David's administrative ability, 15:1–6.

21. Absalom gets David's permission to visit Hebron, Absalom's place of birth and David's first capital. Absalom and his supporters cry "Revolt!" at Hebron, 15:7–11.

22. David's chief counselor, Ahithophel, joins Absalom, 15:12,13.

23. David hears about the revolt, and flees from Jerusalem with his bodyguard, 15:13–18. Though many of his own people have rebelled against him, Ittai the Gittite (who is in charge of David's Philistine mercenaries) remains loyal to him, 15:19–23. David weeps as he leaves Jerusalem, 15:30; see Luke 19:41.

24. David sends Abiathar, Zadok, the Levites and the Ark back to Jerusalem, 15:24–29.

25. David hears that Ahithophel has joined Absalom, 15:31. He sends Hushai back to serve as his "mole" in Absalom's court, 15:32–37. Ziba tells David that Jonathan's son, Mephibosheth, hopes to regain Saul's throne, 16:1–4. David later accepts Mephibosheth's explanation—with some misgivings, 19:24–30.

26. Shimei, a Benjaminite, mocks David as he flees Jerusalem, 16:5–14. Though his bodyguard wants to kill Shimei, David disallows it. David reaches Mahanaim, Ishbosheth's former capital, 17:24–29.

27. Absalom and his supporters enter Jerusalem; Hushai persuades them to let him join them, 16:15–19. Absalom had appointed Amasa, his cousin and David's nephew, to serve as his general, 17:24–26, 1 Chronicles 2:13–17.

28. Ahithophel advises Absalom to have sex with David's concubines, 16:20–23. By doing so, Absalom declares, "I am now the king!"

29. Ahithophel comes up with the perfect plan to establish Absalom on the throne, 17:1–4. Hushai wrecks that plan, 17:5–22.

30. Knowing that David will defeat Absalom and kill him, Ahithophel commits suicide, 17:23. Ahithophel was Bathsheba's grandfather, 11:3, 23:34.

31. Joab kills Absalom in the Forest of Ephraim, ch. 18:1–18. David laments for his son, 18:19–33.

32. David strives to restore a divided and disorganized realm, 19:1–15. David, angry with Joab, appoints Amasa (Absalom's general) as his general (19:13)—a healing, reconciling gesture. David also assures Shimei (a Benjaminite, who cursed him) that he will not seek vengeance, 19:16–23.

33. Jonathan's son assures David he was not plotting to regain the throne, 19:24–30.

34. David places the ten concubines, with whom Absalom slept, in seclusion, 20:3.

35. The Northern Kingdom, led by Sheba, revolts from David, 20:1,2. Amasa, David's new general, is slow-off-the-mark in quelling the revolt, 20:4,5. Abishai is now told to take control of the army, and tells his brother Joab what is taking place. Joab kills Amasa, regains control of the army, and crushes the revolt, 20:6–26.

36. David permits the Gibeonites to put to death two of his brothers-in-law and five of his nephews (Saul's descendants), ch. 21. Note: Merab was Saul's daughter, and a sister to David's wife, Michal. Rizpah had been Saul's concubine, 3:7. He spares Jonathan's son, Mephibosheth, 21:7; note again ch. 9.

37. Chs. 22,23: Hymns of praise, and David's dealings with the Philistines.

38. David conducts a census, is disciplined, and buys the threshing floor of Araunah the Jebusite, on which site Solomon's Temple was eventually built, ch. 24.

D.   David's Last Words and Death (1 Kings 1:1—2:9)

1. David is old and cold, 1:1–4. Abishag, the most beautiful girl in Israel, shares his bed to help keep him warm—and to determine whether he is capable of having sex. Because he is apparently sexually impotent, David can no longer be king.

2. David's son Adonijah assumes he will replace David, and arranges his own coronation, 1:5–10.

3. The prophet Nathan and David's wife Bathsheba persuade David to have another son, Solomon, succeed him, 1:11–31. David has Solomon appointed as his successor, 1:32–40.

4. Adonijah is terrified, and seeks refuge in the Jerusalem sanctuary, 1:41–53.

5. David, prior to his death, gives Solomon some final instructions:

   a. He first instructs Solomon to keep the charge of the Lord, to walk in His ways, and to keep His statutes, commandments, ordinances and testimonies so that the Davidic dynasty might continue, 2:1–4. (This means: *Solomon is to worship one God in Jerusalem!*)

   b. David then asks Solomon to kill Joab (David's nephew and general, and Solomon's cousin) and to kill Shimei (who had cursed him), 2:5–9.

6. David's death is reported in the verses that immediately follow, 2:10–12.

E.   Solomon

1. Adonijah, Solomon's brother, asks to be given David's last-assigned concubine, Abishag the Shunammite. Solomon has Adonijah killed, 1 Kings 2:13–25.

2. Solomon sends the priest, Abiathar, into exile, 1 Kings 2:26–27. Abiathar had supported Adonijah.

3. Solomon has Joab killed, 2:28–35.

4. Solomon has Shimei killed, 2:36–46.

5. Solomon is established as king, 2:46.

6. Reference is made to Solomon's building program and marriage to an Egyptian princess, 3:1.

7. The Temple has not yet been built; all other worship sites (called "high places") are "invalid," 3:2.

8. Solomon worships at shrines other than that in Jerusalem—according to the writers, a bad thing, 3:3. Though the Gibeon shrine is considered invalid, God appears to Solomon there, 3:4,5. *Note the*

references to David's "faithfulness, righteousness, uprightness," 3:6, 11:4,6. These imply: *David worshiped one God in Jerusalem.*

9. Solomon prays for wisdom, 3:7–14. Compare 3:11 with 2:25,34,46, and note how Solomon did not need to ask for the death of his enemies—he has already had them killed!

10. A very important word now appears: "if." The Davidic dynasty will continue *if* (v. 14) his descendants walk in David's ways, which means: They must worship one God in Jerusalem, 3:10–14.

11. Solomon puts his "wisdom" into practice, 3:16–28.

12. Solomon's officials are listed, 4:1–6. He divides the northern part of his realm into twelve districts, and appoints twelve officials to control these, 4:7–19a. He appoints one administrator to have oversight of Judah, 4:19b. Some thought the Messianic Age broke in during Solomon's reign, 4:20; see 4:25.

13. Solomon's borders and needs are described, 4:21–24. Solomon apparently had a large army, which helped control the nation, 4:26,27.

14. More is stated about Solomon's wisdom, 4:29–34.

F.   Solomon and the Building of the Temple

1. Solomon arranges for the building of the Temple—with Phoenician help, 5:1–12.

2. Though Solomon says David was too busy to build the Temple (5:3), 2 Samuel 7:1 says David had "rest" from his enemies, and 2 Samuel 7:4–7 states that God did not want a Temple.

3. Solomon makes use of Israelite "forced labor" for his building projects, 5:13–18.

4. Ch. 6 describes the building, ornamentation and equipping of the Temple; it takes seven years to build, 6:38 (final sentence).

5. It takes thirteen years to complete Solomon's other building projects, 7:1; these are extensive, 7:1–12.

6. Solomon dedicates the Temple, ch. 8. The Ark of the Covenant is placed beneath the wings of the cherubim, 8:6–9. (Note that this narrative was written before the Temple was destroyed in 587 B.C., 8:8.)

7. God bestows divine approval on the Temple, 8:10. (The Holy of Holies had no lighting fixture—it was in darkness, 8:12; note Luke 23:44–46.) The Temple supposedly would stand forever, 8:13.

8. Solomon validates his building of the Temple, 8:14–21. Though he says God had never hitherto chosen a place "for His name" to dwell in, Jeremiah 7:12 insists that God had initially chosen Shiloh, and that *Shiloh was the first place God chose!*

9. Note the "if" in 8:25; the Temple cannot be viewed as a permanent structure, 8:22–26.

10. Indeed, only God's "name" dwells in the Temple, while God lives in heaven, 8:27–30. Possibly the *final* writer was influenced by the destruction of the Temple in 587 B.C., and is making the point that, though the Temple is gone, God is alive and well in heaven.

11. A number of prayers follow; see 8:31–45. The prayer in 8:46–53 suggests that the people are already in exile. When praying, the people are always to face the land, Jerusalem and the Temple, 8:48.

12. 1 Kings 9:1–9 must be read very carefully, and the use of the word "if" in 9:4,6 must be noted. "If" the people worship other gods, they will lose the Davidic dynasty, the land, Jerusalem, the Temple and their status as God's people.

13. Solomon sells Hiram of Tyre twenty Galilean cities to pay his building debts, 9:10–14; 2 Chronicles 8:2 edits this incident somewhat.

14. There is more about Solomon's building ventures, 9:15–22. The writer now suggests that Solomon used only non-Israelites as slaves, while his own people acted as officials and military personnel.

15. Solomon establishes a port city at Ezion-geber in the Gulf of Aqabah, 9:26–28. This gives the Israelites and Phoenicians trading access to countries to the east. After all, at that time there was no Suez Canal!

16. The queen of Sheba visits Solomon (ch. 10), and is most impressed by his court— which is described in lavish terms. Tradition says she became pregnant by Solomon (10:13), and her child became the first king of Ethiopia.

17. An interesting possibility emerges when 1 Kings 10:23–25 is compared with Matthew 2:11; note also Matthew 12:42, 1 Corinthians 1:24. These passages suggest that the visit of the wise men to Jesus had a meaning different from that traditionally applied to it.

18. Apparently Solomon indulged in the arms trade, 10:26–29.

19. Solomon had 700 wives and 300 concubines, 11:1–8. He is not attacked for having 1,000 wives. He is attacked for running after their gods! See 11:4,6, where it stresses that Solomon did not walk in the ways of David; he did not worship one god in one place!

20. Solomon is told that his kingdom will split, 11:9–13. The Northern Kingdom will consist of ten tribes, Judah of one (but see 12:21).

21. Edom (11:14–22) and Syria (11:23–25) break away from Solomon's realm.

22. Jeroboam is told that he will become king of the Northern Kingdom, 11:26–37. His dynasty will last forever, *if he walks in the ways of David*, 11:38. Obviously, he cannot permit his people to continue to worship *in Jerusalem*, since it is in the Southern Kingdom!

23. Solomon tries to have Jeroboam killed, but he escapes by fleeing to Egypt, 11:40.

24. Solomon dies, 11:41–43.

G.   The Kingdom Divides

1. Solomon's son, Rehoboam, automatically gains control of Judah, 11:43. However, he fails to gain control over the Northern part of the realm, 12:1–24. Had he heeded the advice his elders gave him, he might have done so, 12:6,7.

2. Jeroboam is made king of Israel (12:20) and establishes shrines at Bethel and Dan, 12:25–33. Naturally, he cannot permit his people to worship in a capital city (Jerusalem) controlled by another dynasty, and in a Temple beyond his borders.

3. It is likely that the "calves" he set up in Dan and Bethel were copies of the *cherubim* in Solomon's Temple. It is important to note that the *prophets* do not attack these "calves" as "idols."

4. The writers of Kings detest Jeroboam and all Northern kings. They walked in the ways of Jeroboam (1 Kings 12:28,29), the son of Nebat, and did not, like David, worship one God in one place—Jerusalem!

5. The key to understanding the theology of Kings is found in 1 Kings 3:1–5; 11:4,6–8. These passages view any shrine other than the Jerusalem Temple as a "high place" or invalid shrine—including those built before the Temple was constructed.

H.   Josiah

1. The first king who took significant steps to centralize worship in Jerusalem was Hezekiah (715–687 B.C.). The reign of Hezekiah is described in 2 Kings 18:1–20:21. Apparently, he carried out some kind of reform movement, 18:1–8; see also 2 Chronicles 29:1–11 (note vv.5–7); Isaiah 36:7.

2. Hezekiah apparently did not achieve his goal. Possibly any progress he made in this direction was undone by his son Manasseh (687–642), whose son Amon ruled for only two years (642–640) before being killed by "the people of the land," 2 Kings 21:19–26.

3. The reign of Josiah is outlined in 2 Kings chs. 22,23. In 621 B.C., he centralized all worship in Jerusalem—a state of affairs that became the yardstick by which the worth of all kings of Israel and all previous kings of Judah was evaluated.

4. Josiah was a son of Amon (642–640 B.C.). Though Josiah ruled for 31 years (640–609 B.C.), we are told little about his reign, except for a reform that took place in 621 B.C., and his death.

5. Josiah's period of rule is given the highest approval rating, 22:2; 23:24,25.

6. During his reign, repairs on the Temple were undertaken, 22:3–7.

7. During the course of these repairs, a "book of the law" was found and read to Josiah, 22:8–10.

8. Josiah sought an official interpretation of the book's message from Huldah the prophetess, 22:14–20. She said that Judah would be destroyed, but that Josiah would be spared to die in peace. However, Josiah was eventually killed by the Egyptians. 23:28–30.

9. The king played a leading role in a covenant renewal ceremony, 23:1–3. Verse 3 is deserving of careful thought, and what follows throws light on what this piece of Deuteronomic theology means.

10. Josiah now began to reform worship life in Judah (23:4–14), and in what was left of the former Northern Kingdom, 23:15–20.

11. He began by throwing out of the Jerusalem Temple the vessels that had been used for Baal worship and Assyrian astral worship, burning them and throwing their ashes over the shrine at Bethel, 23:4. Bethel had been the royal shrine of the Northern Kingdom, Amos 7:10–13.

12. Two groups of priests are referred to in 2 Kings 23:5, "idolatrous priests" and "those also who worshiped the Baals and the Assyrian astral deities." (The RSV and the NRSV translate correctly here; the NIV misses the point.)

13. Next, he undertook a thorough cleansing of the Jerusalem Temple and its environs, 23:5–14. He did away with Baal worship, Assyrian astral worship, male prostitutes, the weaving of hangings for Asherah, the horses dedicated to the sun, the altars of Ahaz and Manasseh, child sacrifice, and the worship of the gods of neighboring nations (the latter introduced by Solomon).

14. Josiah invited the "idolatrous priests" (referred to in 23:5) to join the staff of the Jerusalem Temple, 23:9. He would not have done so had they been literally idolatrous and pagan.

15. What was wrong with these priests and their shrines was not their *theology*, but their *geography*. Josiah was now centralizing all worship in the Jerusalem Temple.

16. After dealing with Judah, he moved into the former Northern Kingdom where he destroyed all the shrines and killed all the priests, 23:15–20. (It would seem that 1 Kings 13 is a *midrash*, or commentary, on 2 Kings 23:16–18.)

17. Next, Josiah commanded the people to hold a Passover observance in Jerusalem, 23:21–23. The text does not say that the people had not been observing the Passover; they had been doing so. The key word in 23:22 is "such." The point is that, from then on (621 B.C.), the people observed the Passover and all other festivals, and offered all sacrifices, in only one place: Jerusalem. This practice reflected Joshua 5:10–12, where all the people celebrated the Passover in one place, Gilgal.

18. Most likely, the book found in the Temple (22:8–10) was Deuteronomy. The consensus of opinion is that Deuteronomy was used in the Northern Kingdom to spearhead an attempt, sometime just prior to 721 B.C., to centralize all worship in that realm, most likely at Shechem or on nearby Mt. Gerizim. The hope was that such a move would stave off the impending march on Israel by the Assyrians. The Northern Kingdom's "repentance" did not prevent the Assyrian advance. Some of the Northern priests saw the writing on the wall and fled south. They took with them some of their sacred writings, including Deuteronomy, and placed them in the store rooms attached to the Jerusalem Temple. In 621 B.C., workmen repairing the Temple found this "book of the law." Its discovery provided the impetus for Josiah's reform and the centralization of the nation's worship life in Jerusalem.

19. Though Deuteronomy frequently says that the people were to worship their one God in one place, it nowhere attaches a name to that place, Deuteronomy 12:5,11,14,18,21,26; 14:23; 16:2,11. Compare this with Exodus 20:24, where Moses permits the people to worship in many places. As pointed out in point 18 above, most likely the reference in Deuteronomy is to Shechem or Mt. Gerizim. When the book was found in 621 B.C., those who read it *guessed* that the term "the place where the Lord made His name to dwell" meant Jerusalem.

20. Whoever wrote or completed 1 and 2 Kings (and possibly Joshua through 2 Kings) in Babylon (2 Kings 25:27–30, 560 B.C.) based his evaluation of any king from Israel or Judah on his attitude to the Jerusalem Temple. This conviction established itself in 621 B.C.—the time of Josiah's reform. Hence, the writer or editor dismisses all Northern kings as evil. They walked in the ways of Jeroboam, "the son of Nebat, who caused Israel to sin," 23:15. They, like Jeroboam before them, stopped their people from worshiping in the Jerusalem Temple. Only those Southern kings who honored the Jerusalem Temple, and promoted worship within it, could be called "good." *Only they* walked in the ways of David, who worshiped one God in one city, Jerusalem!

21. There is reason to believe that 2 Kings originally ended at 23:25, and that the writer celebrated the idea that Josiah had restored the Davidic Kingdom. However, despite Josiah's reform, Judah was destroyed by the Babylonians—and in 23:26–25:30 the writer outlines Judah's last days. The final four verses of ch. 25 contain a message of hope. King Jehoiachin is still alive—perhaps he will lead the people back to Judah and reestablish the Davidic realm!

22. After the centralization of the sacrificial system in the Temple, provision was made for worshipers from far and near to purchase sacrificial animals inside the Temple precincts. And because only coins bearing no image could be used in making those purchases, money-changers set up shop in the vicinity.

23. There is reason to believe that Josiah's reform set the stage for the situation Jesus had to deal with when He entered Jerusalem five days prior to His death, Mark 11:1–19; Matthew 21:12,13; Luke 19:45–48. Jesus did not attack the Temple as such. He attacked the corrupt practices taking place within it. Jesus' death was not sought by the ordinary people of the land, but by the religious leaders for whom the name of the game was not servanthood, but power and money! What has changed?

DAVID, SOLOMON AND THE TEMPLE IN CHRONICLES

A. The Chronicler's Goal

1. 1 and 2 Chronicles outline the history of humanity and the Israelites from Adam until 587 B.C., as some within the postexilic community understood it. In selecting and editing the events for his writings, the Chronicler sought to give direction to his contemporaries—the continuation of a people that had suffered destruction and exile.

2. His point was: The Babylonian exile was a catastrophe. It must never be permitted to happen again. How can this be achieved? The Israelites must strive to be the kind of people God intended them to be. The Chronicler's purpose was to reveal the ways and actions of the living God in the affairs of humanity at the time he wrote.

3. In the first ten chapters of 1 Chronicles, the writer uses *genealogical tables* to cover the period from the beginning of time to Saul, 9:35–44. The only information the writer gives about events in Saul's life is, ironically, an account of his death, 1 Chronicles 10. The writer shows considerable interest in the tribe of Judah, 1 Chronicles 2:3–17.

4. Remarkably, 1 Chronicles 1–9 make no reference to:

   a. creation
   b. the patriarchal period
   c. the exodus from Egypt
   d. the events at Sinai
   e. the wilderness wanderings
   f. the conquest under Joshua
   g. the period of the judges

5. The Chronicler devotes nineteen chapters to the life of David, 1 Chronicles chs. 11–29. He proposes to establish and defend the legitimate claims of the Davidic monarchy in Israel's history, and to underscore the place of Jerusalem and its divinely established Temple worship as the center of religious life for the Jewish community of his day. If Judaism is to survive and prosper, it will have to heed the lessons of the past and serve God in the one place where God has chosen to dwell—the Jerusalem Temple. From the Chronicler's point of view, David's reign is the ideal to which all subsequent rule in Judah must aspire.

B. The Chronicler's David

1. The Chronicler devotes one chapter to Saul's life, introducing him only to dispose of him, 1 Chronicles 10. Though the description of Saul's suicide follows 1 Samuel 31:1–13 closely, it omits the unpleasant details about the indecent exposure of the bodies of Saul and his sons, and emphasizes the reasons for

Saul's tragic end, 10:13,14. *All of Saul's sons are wiped out at the battle of Gilboa*; this in turn means that David does not have to dispose of them; see 2 Samuel chs. 9 and 21. In short, Saul is seen merely as an obstacle to David's kingship, someone to be removed as quickly as possible.

2. The Chronicler's version of David is very different from that contained in 1 Samuel 16:1 through 1 Kings 2:9. It contains no reference to any of David's sins, but focuses on how David established Israel as a nation, captured Jerusalem and established it as the nation's key religious center, and made every preparation for the construction of the Temple that Solomon eventually built. The writer's central conviction is that the history of Israel (and the world!) took place so that the Jerusalem Temple might be built and the community of Israel might worship the God of Israel within its walls. David himself is considered an almost "ecclesiastical" monarch.

3. The Chronicler gives the impression that Israel's true beginning was not at Sinai with the giving of the Law, but with the rise of David—who is the apple of the Chronicler's eye. He treats the life of David in four blocks of materials:

   a. David is made king of Judah and Israel, chs. 11,12.
   b. David brings the Ark to Jerusalem, chs. 13–16 (ch. 17 parallels 2 Samuel 7).
   c. David expands his realm, chs. 18–20.
   d. David prepares for the building of the Temple, chs. 21–29.

4. In Samuel and Kings, David is presented as a political leader, a man with strengths and weaknesses that endeared him to his people as the greatest king of all Israel. The Chronicler, however, shows only a limited interest in David's political genius. This is understandable, for by the time he wrote, Israel had ceased to be a nation. To be sure, the Chronicler did glory in David's military accomplishments and the splendor of his realm (1 Chronicles chs. 18–20), and emphasized also the Nathan oracle, 1 Chronicles 17; see 2 Samuel 7. However, for the Chronicler, David was primarily the one who organized Israel as a worshiping community. It was David who made Jerusalem, the Holy City, his religious capital. It was David who planned the building of the Temple according to God's directions, 1 Chronicles 28:19. It was David who organized the music of the Temple and assigned the Levites their duties. Although 2 Samuel 6 says that David alone made the decision to bring the Ark of the Covenant into Jerusalem, the Chronicler says the move was sanctioned by all the people, 1 Chronicles 13:1–5.

5. The ecclesiastical robes with which the writer invests David tend to cover David the man. Therefore he does not mention the following:

   a. David's troubles with and flights from Saul, 1 Samuel chs. 18–26.
   b. David's early "Robin Hood"-like career in the wilderness.
   c. David's slaughter of the Amalekites, 1 Samuel 27:8–12.
   d. David's attempt to obtain the favor of Judah's elders, 1 Samuel 30:26–30.
   e. The early wars between Judah and Israel, 2 Samuel 2:12–17; 3:2.
   f. Ishbosheth's period of rule in Israel, 2 Samuel 2:8–10.
   g. Joab's murder of Abner, 2 Samuel 3:22–30.
   h. David's slaughter of Jerusalem's lame and blind, 2 Samuel 5:8.
   i. David's harem, 2 Samuel 3:2–5; 5:13–16; 15:16; 20:3.
   j. David's adultery with Bathsheba and murder of Uriah, 2 Samuel chs. 11,12.
   k. Amnon's rape of Tamar, 2 Samuel 13:1–19.
   l. Absalom's murder of Amnon, and his flight, return, revolt and death, 2 Samuel 13:20–18:33.
   m. Sheba's revolt, 2 Samuel 20.
   n. The murder of Saul's sons and grandsons, 2 Samuel 21.

o. The struggle between Adonijah and Solomon for the throne, 1 Kings ch. 1.

p. David's deathbed instructions to Solomon to kill Joab and Shimei, 1 Kings 2:1–9.

6. The Chronicler declares that, to the very last, David's mind was engrossed with dreams about the future Temple, 1 Chronicles chs. 28,29. The last words the Chronicler attributes to David constitute one of the finest prayers in the Old Testament, 1 Chronicles 29:10–19.

7. It is interesting to note that, according to 2 Samuel 24:24, David bought the real estate on which the Temple would eventually be built for the equivalent of about twenty American dollars. However, according to 1 Chronicles 21:25, he paid the equivalent of 10,000 dollars for it. Similarly, the Chronicler speaks of about 3,775 tons of gold and 37,750 tons of silver being used in the construction of the Temple, 1 Chronicles 22:14. David himself gave, from his personal fortune, the equivalent of 115 tons of gold and a 265 tons of silver for use in the construction of the Temple, 1 Chronicles 29:3,4. The Temple and the ground on which it stands are indeed precious!

C. The Chronicler's Solomon

1. The Chronicler outlines the reign of Solomon with a similar emphasis. So keen is the Chronicler to praise Solomon's reign that he suggests it was even more glorious than David's, 1 Chronicles 29:25; but see 2 Kings 18:5, 23:25.

2. The Chronicler does not mention the following:

   a. Solomon's struggle for the throne, 1 Chronicles 23:1ff; 28:3ff, 29:1,22.

   b. Solomon's use of Israelite slave labor, 2 Chronicles 2:17,18; 8:7–10.

   c. Solomon's gift of twenty Galilean cities to Hiram of Tyre; see 2 Chronicles 8:1,2.

   d. Solomon's many wives; his son, Rehoboam, has numerous wives, 2 Chronicles 11:21.

   e. Solomon's idolatry, 1 Kings 11:1–13; 2 Kings 23:13.

3. Solomon does not permit one of his wives, who is the pharaoh's daughter, to live in Jerusalem, 2 Chronicles 8:11.

4. In relation to the Temple:

   a. 2 Chronicles 3:1 links the Temple site to Mt. Moriah, where Genesis 22:2 says Abraham was to sacrifice Isaac.

   b. The Chronicler suggests that the front porch of the Temple was 180 feet high (Hebrew text), and he nearly doubles the height of the freestanding columns near the Temple's entrance, 2 Chronicles 3:3,4,15. Compare the statistics in 1 Kings 6.

   c. While 1 Kings 6:31 says the Holy of Holies was separated from the Holy Place by doors made of olive wood, the Chronicler says the two areas were separated by a curtain, 2 Chronicles 3:14 (as it was in Herod's Temple, and, most likely, in the postexilic Temple). He also provides Solomon with a platform on which to pray (2 Chronicles 6:13), because in the postexilic period only the priests were permitted to pray before the altar.

D. The Chronicler and the Kings of Israel

1. 2 Chronicles 10–36 deals with the history of the people of God from the time of Solomon's death until the catastrophe of 587 B.C.

2. The writer pays only passing attention to the Northern Kingdom and mentions its history only when he must do so in order to make sense out of the history of Judah. His conviction is that the Northern Kingdom never belonged to the people of God. Why? It had cut itself off from the Davidic dynasty (the only legitimate dynasty) and did not encourage worship in the Temple (the only legitimate shrine) at Jerusalem (the only place in which God made God's name to dwell); see 2 Chronicles 6:5,6 and 13:1–12, especially vv. 5,8. Chronicles does not even mention the Assyrian destruction of the Northern Kingdom in 721 B.C.

E.   The Chronicler and Later Kings of Judah

1. Although the Chronicler idealizes the reigns of David and Solomon, this is not the case with later kings of Judah. What he has to say about the later kings is much influenced by the concept of retribution for neglect of God's will. He sees the fate of each king as related to his religious or irreligious conduct.

2. In 2 Chronicles, kings are rewarded or punished as follows:

    a. Shisack's invasion of Judah is related to Rehoboam's disobedience, 12:2,12.
    b. Asa is afflicted with gangrene soon after unwise behavior, 16:7–12,
    c. Jehoshaphat's maritime ventures fail because they involve fellowship with a Northern king, 20:35–37.
    d. Uzziah is afflicted with leprosy because of his pride, 26:16–23.
    e. It seems inconceivable that God should have permitted a king as wicked as Manasseh to reign for so long; hence, in Chronicles he repents, 33:10–13; see 2 Kings 21:10–16.
    f. Josiah's death at the hands of Pharaoh Neco is not without cause, 35:20–25; see 2 Kings 23:28–30.

3. The point is clear: Do not treat God lightly, for God takes a dim view of disobedience. God treats the nation as God treats its kings. Therefore, be the kind of people you were intended to be!

F.   The Chronicler's Focus: The Temple

1. The work of the Chronicler constitutes a history of Israel's worship life centering on Mt. Zion in Jerusalem. Accordingly, despite the account of David's life in 2 Samuel 16–1 Kings 2:9, the Chronicler says David made preparations for the building of the Temple, planned its worship life, and organized the priestly groups who would function within its walls. He thus looks beyond David to the Temple, and beyond the Temple to God.

2. Why does he do this? The way to avoid a repetition of the exile is to take the God worshiped in the Jerusalem Temple as seriously as possible. If David took such interest in the Temple, postexilic Israel should emulate his example!

3. What does this imply for Israel's spiritual life? To begin with, it is essential that Israel be obedient. The Chronicler stresses this through the manner in which he sets forth Israel's history from Solomon until 587 B.C. To illustrate, 2 Chronicles contains 822 verses, of which 480 describe the reigns of four pious kings and 342 the reigns of seventeen other kings. In doing this, the Chronicler frequently uses words such as "laws," "commandment," "statutes" and terms that have to do with reward and punishment.

4. Furthermore, Israel is called to be a church, a worshiping community, a kingdom of priests and a holy nation, Exodus 19:5,6. It is called to be a people whose life is a liturgy and a divine service. Its activities are to center around the Jerusalem Temple where priests, especially Levites, are to have an indispensable place in the conduct of the worship. Even a cursory reading of the Chronicler's record

shows his interest in liturgical activities. Festival and worship services are frequently described, and the people are always ready to participate in them. For example, the people experience such joy in observing Hezekiah's passover that they decide to observe it a second time the following week, 2 Chronicles 30:23.

5. The Chronicler betrays a particular interest in those people set aside to supervise the worship life of the nation, namely, the priests and Levites. He frequently stresses the importance of their respective roles. They even take part in military ventures. He takes care to distinguish the priests and Levites from the laity, and all earlier references to laymen participating in a religious function or entering a holy area are absent. Accordingly, David's sons are not priests, but officials, 2 Samuel 8:18; 1 Chronicles 18:17. Only priests can take part in the coup which dethrones Athaliah because the event takes place in the Temple, 2 Kings 11:4–20; 2 Chronicles 23.

G.   1 and 2 Chronicles: Miscellaneous Observations

1. In the Chronicler's writings, the focal point in Israel's history shifts from the Exodus to the establishment of the Jerusalem Temple and the inauguration of its worship and rituals.

2. The Chronicler manifests an intense dislike for anything related to the Northern Kingdom. It is possible that he adopts this attitude to prove to the Samaritans the legitimacy of the Davidic dynasty and the worship life centered in the Jerusalem Temple. The Samaritans had cut themselves off from Judah and its worship life about the time the Chronicler was writing.

3. The anti-Northern Kingdom polemic is revealed in numerous ways. When King Abijah of Judah goes to war against Jeroboam I, he delivers a speech prior to the battle. In the speech, Abijah declares it a foregone conclusion that the Northern armies will be defeated—the North does not submit to the Davidic dynasty and has established an illegitimate priesthood, 2 Chronicles 13:4–12. Many from the North flee to the South when they observe that the Lord is with Asa, 2 Chronicles 15:9.

4. The Chronicler shows a greater interest in the tribe of Benjamin than any other except Judah and Levi. In the postexilic period, much of the former territory of Benjamin was attached to Judah, 1 Chronicles 8:1–40; 9:7–9; Nehemiah 11:7–9.

5. Significant comments are made about the Ark of the Covenant and the Tabernacle. However, they are at different locations: the Ark is in Jerusalem and the Tabernacle is at Gibeon, 1 Chronicles 16:1,37–42; 21:28–22:1. The two come together when Solomon dedicates the Temple, 2 Chronicles 5:2–7.

6. The Chronicler's use of numbers gives rise to debate. He seems to take delight in exaggerating the size and glory of the Temple, and, for example, the numbers of people from all Israel who pledged allegiance to David, and the size of David's army and personal bodyguard. His numbers should not be seen as a problem, but as a preliminary glimpse of the grandeur, splendor and abundance that will be Israel's when finally the nation enters the Messianic Age—the focus of all its hopes.

7. Though the monarchy was a thing of the past when the Chronicler wrote, his picture of David is designed to encourage the faithful to look for the time when the promise made to David (2 Samuel 7; 1 Chronicles 17) will be revitalized. When that time comes, David's Messianic descendant will be as little like the previous kings of Judah as possible. Hence, his account of David is a statement about the David that should have been, rather than the David that actually was. Perhaps he is giving his readers a glimpse of the ideal Messianic king many believed would one day come. These points are admittedly hypothetical. It may be that his account of David is meant to focus attention solely on the Temple and, above all, on the God of that Temple.

8. A central concern of the Chronicler's account is to show that Israel can secure its future by continuing to worship God according to the pattern set by David. Hence, the Chronicler presents the Judah of his day as a worshiping community that is a direct extension of the worshiping community God established centuries before through David. Its social and religious structures are those that David created at God's command.

9. Israel's hopes, then, did not reside in what a Messiah might be able to accomplish or reveal sometime in the future. Israel could secure its future by carefully honoring the religious institutions and practices revealed by God to David, handed down to Judah's priests, and kept alive by the remnant that survived the exile and returned to Jerusalem.

10. In the light of the above, the Chronicler viewed the exile as little more than an unfortunate interruption in the otherwise unbroken history of Judah as a worshiping community. In the Chronicler's scheme, the reestablishment of the monarchy was not as important as the reestablishment of the proper worship of God in Jerusalem. The people who supported and worshiped at the Temple fulfilled all the important tasks of the period of the monarchy.

11. When the Chronicler wrote, not all of Abraham's descendants recognized the Jerusalem Temple as the only legitimate place of worship. There was a temple dedicated to the worship of God on Mt. Gerizim in Samaria; the destruction of this temple in 128 B.C. by the Jewish Hasmonean king, John Hyrcanus, led to the final break between Jews and Samaritans.

12. The Chronicler does not see fit to mention the temples Jeroboam established at Bethel and Dan. For him, there could be only one Temple—that in Jerusalem. In his estimation, the Northerners did not have the true priesthood, and their worship was useless, 2 Chronicles 13:9.

Also from Crossways International

❧ Further learning aids for *The Bible's Big Story*

    ❧ a 72" X 22" wall-chart version of the full-color time line
    ❧ a 35" X 12" transparency of the full-color time line
    ❧ a video surveying the biblical narrative on the basis of the time line,
        featuring Dr. Harry Wendt, author of *The Bible's Big Story*

❧ *See Through the Scriptures Video Series* is another visual journey through the Bible's narrative, with a lot of new "scenery": 75 vivid and memorable illustrations. Dr. Harry Wendt uses these to guide you through the Old and New Testaments in sixteen 30-minute video sessions. Each session features an introduction by a moderator, a presentation of a topic by Dr. Wendt, and a wrap-up and question segment. You will be supplied with a colorful 84-page student manual to go along with the video. This series is an excellent basis for personal, family or group study.

❧ *In Heaven's Name, Why on Earth* takes on the issue of Christian management of so-called worldly goods. The Bible teaches that creation is not worldly but sacred. We don't own it, or any portion of it; God does, and we are entrusted to be God's managers of it. What does this mean for "our" assets and "our" lives? This illustrated book guides you to the Bible for answers. You will also be intrigued and inspired by some additional resources: "Ten Deadly Delusions," "The Jesus Chair," and a suggested "Vision for Ministry and Mission" for a church.

To receive more information about Crossways International and our materials and seminars, please call the number at the bottom of the page. Or, fill out the form below, and send it to the address or fax number listed below. We would be happy to send you our free catalogue, featuring Bible study courses, study Bibles, children's Bibles, Christian reference books and other products.

Name _____

Mailing Address _____

City _____ State _____ Zip _____

Telephone (   ) _____ (optional)

        Mail this form to: *Or call or fax at:*

        Crossways International
        7930 Computer Ave. So.   (612) 832-5454 (phone)
        Minneapolis, MN 55435-5415   (612) 832-5553 (fax)
        U.S.A.

PLEASE CONSIDER SHARING WHAT YOU HAVE LEARNED . . .

We read the paper, watch the television news, drive through poor neighborhoods. In the midst of a world that can make us feel sad and helpless, consider this confession of a former Puerto Rican drug king. He ended up in an Alaskan prison, where he attended a seminar designed by Crossways International:

> *Before coming to prison I have dreamed the same dream several times. I saw myself driving up in front of my sister's house in a shiny new car. When I stepped out I was dressed in a fine suit. Everyone was happy to see me because I had become a great success. Now I know that the dream will become a reality, but it will be through Christ that I will clothe myself and become a success in life. It will require His strength . . . all I have to do is "follow Him."*

Every year Crossways International leads thousands of people into the Bible where they discover their God-given mission: to restore people to unity with God and each other through Christ. We are active in more than forty countries—from Liberia, Estonia, Indonesia and Guatemala to churches, schools, prisons and special ministries in North America, Australia and New Zealand.

Wherever we go, we train local pastors and leaders to use our visual and written materials to teach the Bible to members of their community—from the illiterate to the educated. Crossways International's courses are used by more than thirty denominations around the world.

We can do this only because people like you have helped. If you would like someone else somewhere in the world to know and celebrate the wondrous message of the Bible, please consider a donation to Crossways International.

If you are able to send a gift of $30 or more, we would be pleased to send you a special Crossways International leather bookmark as a thank you for your partnership. Please check the appropriate box below.

Yes, I want to be part of the dynamic work of Crossways International to teach the Word of God so people can know Christ and live as His servants. Enclosed is a gift to help meet the needs of this crucial mission.

❑ $150   ❑ $100   ❑ $60   ❑ $30   ❑ other _____

❑ My gift is $30 or more; please send me the special Crossways International leather bookmark.

Please print the following information (if not included on your check).

Name _____

Street _____

City _____   State _____   Zip_____

Telephone (_____) _____ (optional)

Please cut off this portion of the page and mail it with your check (payable to **Crossways International**) to:
Crossways International
7930 Computer Ave. So.
Minneapolis, MN 55435-5415
U.S.A.

We are grateful for your prayers, encouragement and generous support.

Crossways International is a nonprofit organization. Contributions from U.S. donors are tax deductible.